THE MUSCOVY MERCHANTS OF 1555

THE

MUSCOVY MERCHANTS

OF 1555

BY

T. S. WILLAN

[1953]

AUGUSTUS M. KELLEY • PUBLISHERS

CLIFTON 1973

First Edition 1953

(*Manchester*: Manchester University Press, 1953)

REPRINTED 1973 BY

AUGUSTUS M. KELLEY · PUBLISHERS

REPRINTS OF ECONOMIC CLASSICS

CLIFTON NEW JERSEY 07012

Library of Congress Cataloging in Publication Data

Willan, Thomas Stuart.
    The Muscovy merchants of 1555.

    (Reprint of economic classics)
    Includes bibliographical references.
    1. Russia Company, London. 2. London--Commerce--
History. 3. Merchants, British. I. Title.
HF3510.L8W5 1972   382'.0942   72-85754
ISBN 0-678-00929-5

PRINTED IN THE UNITED STATES OF AMERICA
by SENTRY PRESS, NEW YORK, N. Y. 10013

CONTENTS

ABBREVIATIONS

Add. MSS. . . . Additional Manuscripts.

A.P.C. . . . . . *Acts of the Privy Council.*

Beaven . . . . . A. B. Beaven, *The aldermen of the city of London.*

Blake . . . . . J. W. Blake, ed. *Europeans in West Africa, 1450–1560,* Hakluyt Society, second series, lxxxvi, lxxxvii.

Boyd . . . . . P. Boyd, *Roll of the Drapers' Company of London.*

Burgon . . . . J. W. Burgon, *The life and times of Sir Thomas Gresham.*

Carr . . . . . C. T. Carr, ed. *Select charters of trading companies, 1530–1707,* Selden Society, xxviii.

Clode . . . . . C. M. Clode, *The early history of the Guild of Merchant Taylors.*

C.P.R. . . . . . *Calendar of Patent Rolls.*

C.S.P.D. . . . . *Calendar of State Papers Domestic.*

C.S.P. For. . . . *Calendar of State Papers Foreign.*

D.N.B. . . . . . *Dictionary of National Biography.*

E.H.R. . . . . . *English Historical Review.*

Exch. K.R. . . . Exchequer, King's Remembrancer.

Hakluyt . . . . R. Hakluyt, *The principall navigations, voiages and discoveries of the English nation* (Everyman edition).

Harl. MSS. . . . Harleian Manuscripts.

Hasted . . . . . E. Hasted, *History of Kent.* Part 1. The Hundred of Blackheath, ed. H. H. Drake.

H.C.A. . . . . . High Court of Admiralty.

H.M.C. . . . . . *Historical Manuscripts Commission.*

Inq. p.m. Lond. . . *Abstracts of Inquisitiones post mortem relating to the city of London.* (Index Library, vols. 15, 26, 36.)

Johnson . . . . A. H. Johnson, *The history of the worshipful Company of the Drapers of London.*

Lambert . . . . J. J. Lambert, ed. *Records of the Skinners of London, Edward I to James I.*

Lans. MSS. . . . Lansdowne Manuscripts.

Machyn	*The diary of Henry Machyn*, ed. J. G. Nichols, Camden Society, xlii.
Marsden	R. G. Marsden, ed. *Select pleas in the Court of Admiralty*, Selden Society, vi, xi.
Morgan and Coote .	E. D. Morgan and C. H. Coote, eds. *Early voyages and travels to Russia and Persia*, Hakluyt Society, lxxii, lxxiii.
Nicholl	J. Nicholl, *Some account of the worshipful Company of Ironmongers.*
Overall	W. H. and H. C. Overall, *Analytical index of the series of records known as the Remembrancia preserved among the archives of the city of London.*
P.C.C.	Prerogative Court of Canterbury.
Return	*Return of Members of Parliament* (1878).
Smit	H. J. Smit, ed. *Bronnen tot de geschiedenis van den handel met Engeland, Schotland en Ierland, 1485–1585.*
S.P.	State Papers.
S.P.D.	State Papers Domestic.
Stow	J. Stow, *A survey of London*, ed. C. L. Kingsford.
Strype	J. Stow, *A survey of London*, ed. J. Strype. London, 1720.
T.R.H.S.	*Transactions of the Royal Historical Society.*
V.C.H.	*Victoria County History.*

CHAPTER I

THE SETTING

ENGLISH society in the sixteenth century was at once hierarchical and fluid. It possessed a theoretical rigidity which assigned to men their proper places in the social structure and a practical flexibility which allowed them to move up or down the social scale. Such movements no doubt impaired the ideal of a well-ordered society, but even without them it was not always easy to assign some men to their proper places within the social hierarchy. Such a difficulty arose in the case of the merchant. It arose partly from the nature of the contemporary classification into which he had to be fitted and partly from the wide diversity within his occupational group. The conventional gradations of labourer, husbandman, yeoman, gentleman, esquire, and knight were more applicable to rural than to urban life, and the merchant was usually a townsman. Moreover the term 'merchant' was not clearly defined. Even if it were limited to those engaged in foreign trade, it could still embrace a very wide group, whose members ranged from the provincial merchant, who might also be a tradesman and even a handicraftsman, to the great merchant princes of London. It is not surprising therefore that the merchant was not easily classified or easily fitted into the hierarchical structure of sixteenth-century society.

The merchant had not only an uncertain place in the social structure, he had also an uncertain place in the opinions of his articulate contemporaries. His cool secular approach to economic matters disturbed those who regarded usury as a damnable sin. His operations in time and space disturbed those who regarded middlemen as the caterpillars of the commonwealth. His import of luxury goods disturbed statesmen who regarded a favourable balance of trade as an essential element in national power. On the other hand the merchant's operations led to an accumulation of wealth which could be tapped by the crown. Moreover such operations, when they involved trade with foreign countries, seemed less perverse than the machinations of middlemen engaged in internal trade, who were alleged to corner the market and to raise the price of foodstuffs. Again, the merchant as an exporter of English manufactures was felt not only to be providing employment, especially in the cloth industry, but also to be providing the basis for a favourable trade balance by which the bullion of the country might be increased. Thus the wealth and activities of the larger merchants impressed contemporaries who saw in them a sign of national prosperity and greatness. The Lawyer in Wilson's *Discourse upon usury* saw in the merchants' wealth 'the welfare of the realme'. After exposing the iniquities of the mere retailer, he extolled the virtues of the merchant adventurer who 'is and maye be taken for a lordes fellow in dignitie'.[1] Similarly Thomas Lodge, the poet, thought that 'no well governed state' could exist without merchants, who brought in 'store of wealth from forrein nations', but who also enriched 'themselves mightelye by others misfortunes' and ate 'our English gentrie out of house and home'.[2]

Some who realized that merchants played a necessary role in the national economy nevertheless believed that they were becoming too numerous. Thus Harrison thought that their number had so increased 'that theire onelie maintenance is the cause of the exceeding prices of forreine wares', and he wished that 'the huge heape of them were somewhat restreined'.[3] Cecil himself viewed the restoration of trade with Antwerp in 1564 with some misgiving as 'the shortnes of the retorn multeplyeth manny marchantes, and so consequently also this realme is overburdened with unnecessary forrayn wares'.[4] It is difficult to

---

[1] T. Wilson, *A discourse upon usury*, ed. R. H. Tawney, p. 203.

[2] T. Lodge, *An alarum against usurers*, ed. E. W. Gosse, pp. 13–14.

[3] W. Harrison, 'Description of England', in R. Holinshed, *Chronicles*, ed. 1807, i. 274.

[4] R. H. Tawney and E. Power, *Tudor economic documents*, ii. 45.

say whether these complaints of the increased numbers of merchants were justified. Biased observers, like the Russia Company when applying for a statutory confirmation of its monopoly in 1566, could maintain that ' of late yeres almoste everye yonge mane of what occupation or scyens soever he be, if he be abell to make xx or xxx pound stock, will over the sea and be a marchant '.[1] Such statements were however part of the stock-in-trade arguments of those who wished to obtain or maintain their trading monopolies. Few attempted any statistical estimate of the number of merchants either in London or in the country as a whole, though Wheeler made the rash statement that there were 3500 members of the Merchant Adventurers' Company in 1601.[2] Half a century earlier, according to Strype, there had been ' but few English Merchants Adventurers ', but the numbers had increased until by 1561 there were ' in all 327 ' merchants in London. It seems a modest estimate.

Most contemporaries, when they thought of merchants as men essentially engaged in foreign trade, thought also of them as Londoners. There were probably two inter-connected reasons for this emphasis on the metropolitan merchant—the part played by London in the foreign trade of the country and the part played by the London merchant in the foreign trade of his city. London was ' the principall store house and staple of all commodities within this realme '.[4] It was also the funnel through which most of the foreign trade of the country passed. Exactly what proportion of England's foreign trade passed through London, it is impossible to say. The surviving official statistics do not allow of a reliable estimate, partly because they are incomplete and partly because they take no account of smuggling, which may have been considerable, especially at the outports where the customs administration was probably laxer[5] than in

[1] S. P. D. Eliz., xl. no. 93.
[2] J. Wheeler, *A treatise of commerce* (Facsimile Text Society), p. 57.
[3] Strype, ii. bk. v. 291.   [4] Stow, i. 12.
[5] On this point see N. J. Williams, ' Francis Shaxton and the Elizabethan Port Books ', *E.H.R.* lxvi. 387–95.

London. Such figures as exist certainly suggest the overwhelming preponderance of London. Thus in the year ending Michaelmas 1544 London handled almost 87 per cent of the country's most important export, cloth.[1] In the year from Michaelmas 1559 to Michaelmas 1560 the total receipts from the custom and subsidy on cloth and the new imposition on wines amounted to £50,705 of which London accounted for £44,557 or 88 per cent.[2] Finally in the year ending at Michaelmas 1569 London paid 93 per cent of the customs on cloth exports.[3]

This canalization of the stream of trade through London gave a special interest and significance to the city's merchant class. The large volume of trade passing through the port made possible a greater specialization among the merchants. It was perhaps not so much a specialization by commodities or countries as a specialization of the function of the merchant, which differentiated him more clearly than elsewhere from the retailer and the handicraftsman. It is significant that the attempts of the chartered companies to confine their membership to ' mere merchants ', who should be neither retailers nor handicraftsmen, resulted in conflicts, not in London, but in some of the outports. In the provincial ports with their smaller volume of trade the functions of the merchant and the retailer appear often to have been combined, and the retailer could make good his claim to belong to a branch of a company whose official policy had aimed at excluding him. Indeed a study of the customs records suggests that at the smaller ports there was just not sufficient foreign trade to enable those who engaged in it to earn a living by that alone. In London, on the other hand, it was possible for a large class of merchants to arise whose main interest—perhaps whose sole interest—was in foreign trade. Among this class were to be

---

[1] G. Schanz, *Englische Handelspolitik*, ii. 86–7, 102–3.

[2] S.P.D. Eliz., xxx. no. 8.

[3] Ibid., lviii. no. 26. Mr. L. Stone wrongly quotes this document as relating to the year 1559–60 (' Elizabethan Overseas Trade ', *Economic History Review*, 2nd series, ii. 39.)

found the great merchant princes of the city. Such men provided the initiative for the formation of the chartered trading companies and ruled those companies once they had been formed. Among such companies chartered in the sixteenth century the Russia Company has a special interest. Its membership is worth consideration not only because a study of it may throw some light on the merchant class as a whole, but also because the company itself had two features which, taken together, distinguished it from its contemporaries. It was a company formed to open up a new trade and it was a joint-stock company.

The middle years of the sixteenth century saw the development of several new branches of foreign trade. To the south syndicates of merchants were opening up trade with Barbary and the Guinea coast and, in the slaving voyages, extending their operations across the Atlantic. Such trade involved an infringement of the Portuguese and Spanish spheres of influence for, as Robert Thorne had pointed out in an address intended for Henry VIII, of the four parts of the world, the south, south-east, and south-west were already in theory monopolized.[1] There remained only the north to which the English could go freely. No one, however, wanted the north for its own sake, but merely as a passage to the gold and spices of the east. Thus the voyage of 1553, which led to the incorporation of the Russia Company, was really an attempt to find the north-east passage to the Indies. The three ships which left England in May 1553 carried letters addressed to ' all kings, princes, rulers, judges, and governours of the earth ',[2] which suggests a certain vagueness of destination. Instead of finding the north-east passage the ships reached the White Sea and established trading connexions with Russia. Two years later the pioneers of the enterprise were formally incorporated in what became known conventionally as the Russia Company. Thus the members of the company were concerned with developing a new trade, along a new and naturally hazardous route, with a country where their activities depended

[1] Hakluyt, i. 214 ; E. G. R. Taylor, *Tudor geography, 1485–1583*, pp. 46–52, 246.
[2] Hakluyt, i. 241.

on the whims of a despotic ruler. It may well be asked who were the men who pioneered such an enterprise and whether they were the same men who were taking similar risks on the coast of Africa.

From the very first this enterprise had been financed on a joint-stock basis. The initial capital of £6000 is said to have been raised by 240 men subscribing £25 each. It seems impossible to confirm the statement, for which Clement Adams is the sole authority,[1] that the original members numbered 240, but the initial subscription does seem to have been £25.[2] This was raised before the company received its charter, for the grant of a charter was delayed by the last illness and death of Edward VI. The subsequent financial history of the company is exceedingly obscure, but two things are clear. Firstly the company was a joint-stock company in which, for two decades at least, the capital was permanent in the sense that it was not redistributed either after the annual voyages or after a series of such voyages, as was the case in the early years of the East India Company. Secondly, additional capital was raised by making calls on existing shareholders. Thus by 1564 calls of £175 per share had been made.[3] Further calls of £50 in 1570 and £200 in 1572[4] raised the par value of the shares to £450, of which £425 represented calls and £25 represented the original subscription. By 1572, therefore, a member who had met all his calls, had invested a considerable sum in the company.

This method of financing the trade, and indeed the very fact that the Russia Company was a joint-stock company, raise some interesting points in connexion with its membership. Members did not participate in the trade so directly or so actively as they would have done if the company had been a regulated one. In the regulated company the members traded with their own capital employing, where necessary, their own factors and themselves controlling the scale of their operations, subject in

---

[1] Hakluyt, i. 267.
[2] Cecil, for example, recorded the payment of his £25 (Lans. MSS. 118, f. 52).
[3] S.P.D. Eliz., xxxv. no. 20.   [4] Ibid., cviii. no. 63.

some cases to any limitation or stint imposed by the company. In the joint-stock company the members did not trade individually, or at least were not supposed to do so. The company traded as a body, using paid employees who acted as agents and factors. Such employees were employed and paid by the company, not by its individual members. The members were merely shareholders who exercised control through the general assembly and through the court of assistants, which seems to have acted as a sort of board of directors. Thus most members of the Russia Company had probably little say in the day-to-day conduct of business. They were investors, investing in a form of enterprise new to this country, and therefore of interest not only as pioneers in the opening up of a new trade, but also as pioneers in the development of a new financial device for the conduct of that trade.

It is of course true that the Guinea and slaving voyages were conducted on a joint-stock principle, but the groups of merchants who financed those voyages were not incorporated and the capital they subscribed appears to have been redistributed at the end of each voyage. That was not the case with the Russia Company, at least during the early years of its existence. There the capital was more permanent, though it is not clear what happened to shareholders who could not or would not meet the calls made by the company on their shares. Nor is it clear whether such shares were freely transferable, though they could certainly be bequeathed by will. Indeed the evidence of wills suggests that investment in the company was sometimes regarded as being almost in the nature of a trustee stock. Thus William Lewkner, in his will dated 20 November 1558,[1] left his stock in the company to his two sons, stipulating that it should remain for their use until they attained their majorities. Similarly John Kempe, in his will dated 13 September 1569,[2] stated that he held stock in the company on behalf of his nephew. This stock was not to be sold, but was to be retained until the nephew was 24 years old. In the meantime the ' yearly increase ' was to

[1] P.C.C. 21 Welles.   [2] P.C.C. 23 Sheffeld.

be used by Kempe's executors to meet the cost of bringing up his nephew and to pay the company £5 p.a. in return for a true annual account of such increase. Thus the company's stock could be held on behalf of minors and the increase or interest could be used for their maintenance.

The way in which the company conducted its trade and the form in which it raised its capital suggest the question whether its members were rentiers or active merchants, and whether they were the same sort of people, or indeed the same people, who traded to other countries under different conditions. Only an investigation of the company's membership can provide an answer to that question and give some picture, however imperfect, of a group of men important in the commercial life of London.

CHAPTER II

THE CHARTER MEMBERS

THE Russia Company was granted its charter on 26 February 1555.[1] The charter empowered the company to trade with any part of the world ' before the sayd late adventure or enterprise unknowen,[2] and by our marchants and subjects not commonly frequented '. In addition it gave the company a monopoly of the trade with Russia and with all lands ' lying northwards, northeastwards, or northwestwards ', which had not previously been known or commonly frequented by English merchants. The company was to have a common seal, perpetual succession, and the right to hold property value £66 13s. 4d. p.a. It was to be governed by one or two governors, four consuls, and twenty-four assistants, who together could make acts and ordinances ' for the government, good condition, and laudable rule ' of the company and could punish those who offended against such ordinances. The first governor, consuls, and assistants were named in the charter. Except for the governor, Sebastian Cabot, who was appointed for life, they were to hold office for one year and their successors were to be chosen by the company as a whole. On Cabot's death the company was to choose ' one governour or two ' annually.

The members of the company, who were all named in the charter, numbered 201.[3] Their names were given, as might be

---

[1] Patent Rolls, 1 & 2 Philip and Mary, pt. 3. The charter is printed, but without the full list of members, in Hakluyt, i. 318–29, where it is wrongly dated 6 Feb. It is calendared with the full list of members in *C.P.R. 1554–5*, pp. 55–9.

[2] I.e. the first voyage of 1553.

[3] The only other list of members which has survived is one dated May 1555 which gives 205 names (S.P.D. Addenda, Mary, vii. no. 39). It is printed with many inaccuracies in A. J. Gerson, ' The organisation and early history of the Muscovy Company ', in *Studies in the history of English commerce in the Tudor period*, pp. 116–20.

expected, roughly in order of precedence.[1] The list was headed by seven peers, William, marquis of Winchester, lord high treasurer, Henry, earl of Arundel, lord steward of the household, John, earl of Bedford, lord keeper of the privy seal, William, earl of Pembroke, William, lord Howard of Effingham, lord high admiral, William, lord Paget of Beaudesert, and Thomas, lord Darcy. Then followed six knights and two esquires who all held important offices, Sir John Gage, lord chamberlain of the household, Sir Robert Rochester, comptroller of the household, Sir Henry Jerningham, vice chamberlain, Sir William Petre and Sir John Bourne, principal secretaries, Sir Edward Waldegrave, master of the wardrobe, Edward Griffin, esquire, attorney general, and William Cordell, esquire, solicitor general. The list continued with fourteen knights, of whom four were also aldermen, Nicholas Wotton, clerk and doctor in civil law, seven aldermen who were not knights, eleven esquires, and eight gentlemen. Of the remaining 145 members, 144 were arranged in the contemporary fashion in the alphabetical order of their Christian names and were all described as merchants of London. They included two women, inevitably widowed. The list ended with Edward Pryme, citizen and merchant of Bristol, who was the sole mercantile representative from the provinces.

It cannot be said that this was a typical list of members of a sixteenth-century trading company. It was, so to speak, too heavy at the top. The presence of so many peers and holders of high office was quite unprecedented. Such men did not figure among the membership of the Merchant Adventurers' or the Staplers' Company. It is true that later in the century Leicester, Walsingham, and Sir James Croft were charter members of the Spanish Company of 1577[2] and Leicester and Warwick were members of the Barbary Company of 1585,[3] but

---

[1] The spelling of the names of members presents some difficulties, as usual in this period. To adhere rigidly to the spelling used in the charter would involve referring to Cecil as Cicille, Gresham as Gressham, etc. It seems better to give the names in their more modern forms (Young for Yong, Mallory for Mallorie, etc.), but complete consistency in these matters seems impossible.

[2] Patent Rolls, 19 Eliz., pt. 8.   [3] Hakluyt, iv. 268.

two or three peers and office holders do not constitute the sort of galaxy that adorned the Russia Company. Whether these men did much more than adorn the company it is difficult to say, but they may well have proved useful friends at court. On 22 January 1555 the Privy Council sent to the attorney general and the solicitor general 'certayn articles' upon which the company's charter was to be based, requiring them 'to cause a booke to be conceyved and drawen to that effecte'. The 'booke' was to be prepared and sent as quickly as possible so that the Privy Council could 'procure their majesties signature therunto'. Of the seven privy councillors who signed the letter, five were to be charter members of the company, as were the attorney general and solicitor general.[1] There is no evidence however that these peers and office holders took any active part in the company's affairs after the charter had been obtained. One or two of them were interested in other branches of foreign trade. Pembroke was one of the promoters of Hawkins's second slaving voyage of 1564.[2] Darcy, before his elevation to the peerage, had been owner of the *James*, a ship engaged in Iceland fishing.[3] The rest seem to have had no direct connexion with trade.

It is tempting to see in these men the real rentier element among the company's members, but that may be to look at the matter too much through modern eyes. It is, however, difficult to believe that their presence was unconnected with the fact that the company was a joint-stock company in which they could invest their capital without having to play any active part in the management of the trade. The joint-stock form may thus have attracted capital from men who were not interested in investing in branches of trade which required a direct and active participation.

The members of the Russia Company who were neither peers nor holders of high office present a difficult problem of indentification. Knights and aldermen, esquires and gentlemen,

---

[1] *H.M.C. Laing*, i. 13.
[2] J. A. Williamson, *Sir John Hawkins*, p. 92.   [3] Marsden, ii. 6–7.

can usually be identified fairly easily, but the same cannot be said of the large group described as merchants of London. In a few cases the charter described members of this group more specifically. Thus John Harrison was described as 'goldsmith', John Lewes as 'notary public', Thomas Starke as 'draper', and Thomas Nicholes the elder as 'mercer'. Unfortunately such descriptions were rare and 130 of the members were recorded in the charter by name alone, apart from the general statement that they were London merchants. Robert Brown and Thomas Smith are not very communicative names in the sixteenth or any other century. Most members, fortunately, had more distinctive names than these and it is possible to identify some of them from their names alone, though there is admittedly always an element of risk in doing so. Other contemporary evidence, including wills and the 'lapidary scrawl', has brought some of the dead names to life. In all it is possible to identify about half of the members of the company and to make a reasonable guess at the identity of another quarter. It is also possible to discover sufficient about these men to give some picture of their origins and interconnexions, their economic activities and their worldly success.

Though most members of the company were described as merchants of London, a good many of them were not Londoners by birth. That movement of the people which the Tudors deplored and tried to check was nevertheless a reality. London acted as a magnet for the ambitious and the adventurous as, in a different way, did the sea. It was not only the court that attracted men to London, but also the whole commercial life of the city, which offered greater opportunities for rapid and spectacular advancement than were to be found in the provinces.[1] No doubt many failed to profit from these opportunities, failed even to make a tolerable living, and sank down anonymously into the London underworld, but enough succeeded to make some mark on the city of their adoption.

[1] It is interesting to note how many deponents in High Court of Admiralty cases had been born in the provinces and had come up to London in their teens.

For some members of the Russia Company, who began their lives in the provinces, the migration to London did not involve a very long journey even by sixteenth-century standards. The capital naturally attracted migrants from nearby counties. Thus Sir Andrew Judde was born at Barden near Tonbridge, Kent, and went to London as a boy to be apprenticed to John Buknell, skinner and merchant of the staple. John Rivers also came from Kent. Sir Thomas White was born at Reading and was apprenticed at the age of 12 to a London merchant tailor, Hugh Acton. From Suffolk came Roger Martin, Nicholas Bacon, and perhaps Edmund Stile, who declared in his will that he had been brought up at Hadleigh in that county. Further afield, Norfolk supplied the Greshams, the Woodhouses, Ralph Greneway, and Robert Dawbeney. From the west midlands came Clement Throckmorton of Haseley, Warwickshire, Humphrey Baskerfeld, who was born at Wolverley near Kidderminster, and Thomas Offley, who was born at Stafford and who reached London by way of Chester to which his father had migrated. Within this area Shropshire contributed two important names, Thomas Lodge who was born at Cound and Rowland Heyward who was born and educated at Bridgnorth. Further west were the native counties of Philip Gunter, who was born in Monmouthshire, and Stephen Borough, who, as befitted a courageous seaman, came from Devon, the home also of David Woodroff. Wiltshire supplied William Merick, a distinguished servant as well as a member of the company.

These first-generation Londoners often rose to positions of wealth and eminence. It was a case of the local boy making good in the big city, but it is doubtful whether it was often a case of the really poor boy making his fortune. The exact social class from which these boys came is difficult to determine. Few of them seem to have been sons of gentry, though Andrew Judde came of a family of Kentish gentry. The evidence seems too slight for generalization but it rather suggests that it was middle-class provincial families who sent their sons to London. Thus the father of John Rivers was the steward of Edward, duke of Buckingham. Sir Thomas White's father was a clothier. After migrating from Stafford the Offleys became a prosperous Chester family and were benefactors to the city. Others, such as Christopher Draper, Lionel Duckett, John Marshe, and William Hawtrey, appear to have had a more landed background, but it is difficult to be very certain about this.

Whatever their origin these first-generation Londoners were assimilated into the life of their adopted city, and they and other members of the company seem often to have been bound together by ties other than the rather shadowy bond implied by a common membership of the company itself. The strongest and most direct ties were probably those of blood and marriage. Such ties are not always easy to discover even though the age had something of a passion for genealogy. It seems clear however that many of the important merchants were related, either closely or distantly, just as were many of the great Elizabethan seamen. Thus three of the children of Sir George Barne married members or relatives of members of the company. A son George married Anne, daughter of Sir William Garrard. A daughter Elizabeth married John Rivers and another daughter, Anne, married firstly Alexander Carleill and secondly Sir Francis Walsingham, who was himself later a member of the company. The case of the three daughters of Humphrey Packington, who himself had no connexion with the company, is perhaps more striking. They contrived to marry four members of the company and the brother of a member. Letitia married Roger Martin, Jane married firstly Humphrey Baskerfeld and secondly Lionel Duckett, and Anne married firstly Edward Jackman and secondly James Bacon, brother of Sir Nicholas. A cousin of these women, Anne, daughter of Robert Packington, married Richard Mallory. Members were also related through the marriages of their children. Thus Henry Becher's son William married Judith, the daughter of John Quarles, and Christopher Draper's daughter Bridget married David Woodroff's son Stephen. In some cases members were related, but it is impossible now to discover exactly what the relationship was. Thus

Thomas Bannister was related to the Gamages through his wife, but his exact relationship to Anthony Gamage is uncertain.[1] Apart from the relationship based on blood and marriage, there were other ties which may have bound together members of the Russia Company. Some were associated together in civic duties. At least 28 of the members were or became aldermen of London and 16 of them reached the position of lord mayor. This was perhaps less a sign of cohesion within the group than a sign of the wealth and standing of individual members of it. It is some evidence both of individual initiative and of an environment favourable to the exercise of that initiative that 15 aldermanic and 10 mayoral members of the company were first-generation Londoners. The Dick Whittington tradition was by no means dead. Besides playing a part in local government members were concerned in national government as well, for at least 32 of them were at one time or another members of the house of commons. This again was a sign of standing rather than of common ties. Finally some members held office under the crown. The holders of high office may have constituted a definite group among the members but, as has been suggested, their presence was exceptional and the part they played in the company's affairs of doubtful significance. It is not clear what significance should be attached to the holding of lesser offices except as throwing some light on the activities and interests of members who were not primarily merchants.

These office-holders fall roughly into three groups. There were first of all the financial agents of the crown who were concerned with foreign borrowing and for whom a knowledge both of the international money market and of foreign trade was important. Half a dozen members of the company were at one time or another engaged in this work. They were John Dymocke, Sir John Gresham the elder and his nephew Thomas Gresham, Sir William Dansell under whom Thomas Gresham had served as an assistant and who was removed in 1551 'from his office of agent by reason of his slackness', and Christopher

[1] P.C.C. 1 Carew.

Dauntsey, who succeeded Thomas Gresham for a short time as agent on Mary's accession but who proved inefficient, borrowing at an unnecessarily high rate of interest. All these men were what might be called the regular financial agents of the crown. In addition Edward Castelin was sent into Germany in 1576 to raise a loan for the queen.

The second group of officials were those connected with the customs administration. The members of this group are more difficult to identify. They included Sir Richard Blount, who was appointed collector of the great and petty custom and subsidy of Southampton in October 1552, Sir Henry Jerningham, who was appointed 'solicitor and supervisor of kerseys' in the ports of London and Southampton in 1553, and William Clifton, Thomas Colshill, and Edmund Lomnour, all customs officials of London. They seem also to have included Robert Dove, Richard Patrickes, Francis Robinson, Thomas Smith, and Richard Young. Finally a group of members held at one time or another offices in the Mint. Again the exact composition of this group is not certain, but it apparently included Sir John York, who had been master of the Mint, Thomas Egerton, an under-treasurer, and William Humfrey, William Knight, Thomas Gravesend, and William Billingsley, assay masters.

Participation in the government of London as aldermen or in the government of the country as members of parliament and as office-holders does not perhaps throw much light on the affiliations of the members of the company one with another. It was probably in the groupings more integrated with the commercial life of the city, and especially in the livery companies, that closer ties were to be found. It was by apprenticeship to members of such companies that boys secured their professional training and later gained the freedom of the company and the freedom of the city. Such a course was essential for boys who had come in from the provinces, for they could not secure their freedom by patrimony. Even so it is not clear whether membership of a specific livery company had much economic significance in this period for those whose main interest was in foreign trade, especially as the custom of London allowed men to transfer from one occupation to another. Although much work has been done on the London livery companies there is still need for an investigation of the exact significance to be attached to membership of them in the sixteenth century and for a study of their relationship to the increasing number of chartered trading companies.

Most members of the Russia Company, who can be identified and who were not peers or high office-holders, belonged to a livery company. At least 13 were members of the Mercers Company of whom 5 became masters. Ten belonged to the Drapers Company including 4 masters and 8 to the Grocers Company including 2 masters. The Merchant Tailors claimed 7 members of whom 4 became masters, the Skinners 6 including 3 masters, the Haberdashers 5 with only one master, and the Ironmongers 4 including 3 masters. Other companies, the Clothworkers, Fishmongers, Goldsmiths, Pewterers, and Vintners claimed one or two members each. Such a quantitative approach does not however tell the full story, for many of these men were very important figures in the life of their companies in which they repeatedly held the highest offices. Thus Sir Lionel Duckett was four times master of the Mercers and Sir Richard Mallory held the same office three times. Sir William Chester was at least five times master of the Drapers,[1] an office Sir John Branche held four times. The record seems to have been shared between Christopher Draper, who was eight times master of the Iron-mongers, and Philip Gunter, who was eight times master of the Skinners. Gunter's performance was rather better than Sir Andrew Judde's, for Judde was only six times master of the Skinners. In that respect at least the boy from Monmouthshire beat the boy from Kent. Again it is noticeable that many of these men who were prominent in the life of their companies were first-generation Londoners.

[1] Beaven, ii. 34 says he was five times master and Johnson, ii. 106 n., quotes this without comment, but Johnson's list of Masters (ii. 470–1) implies that Chester was seven times master.

Whatever the exact significance to be attached to membership of these companies—and surely it was social as well as economic—the companies themselves seem to have held a high place in the affections of their members. The stream of bequests that flowed into the companies from deceased members shows this.[1] The legacies of plate and of money are a striking testimony of the regard which members felt for their company and it is perhaps not fanciful to see in these companies one of the strongest bonds uniting together the London merchants.

Two further bonds may be considered, the participation of members in common business enterprises and the elusive ties of friendship. Members were grouped together in the pursuit of certain branches of foreign trade, but such groupings are best considered in connexion with the general trading activities of the members. Apart from trade, members were associated in the buying and selling of land. This was often a straightforward transaction between two members of the company. Thus in January 1556 Philip Bold was given licence to grant former chantry property in Wolverhampton to Thomas Offley.[2] Three years later he alienated messuages in London to Miles Mording.[3] There were many similar cases but they do not necessarily imply any closer relationship between the parties than in the sale of property to-day. On the other hand there were transactions in which a number of the members of the company were joined together. Thus in February 1560 Sir Robert Peckham was granted licence to alienate the manor of Godney, Somerset, to Thomas Colshill, Thomas Lodge, Edmund Martin, Miles Saundz, Thomas Smith, and Lionel Duckett.[4] Here at least three members of the company were joined together. Ten years earlier, in February 1550, licence had been given to a group of men to grant their purparties in the manor of Bozeat, Northants, to John and Alice Marshe. The group included Anthony Hickman, Thomas Gresham, Thomas Heton, Thomas Goodman,

---

[1] For a fuller consideration of these bequests see below pp. 64–6.
[2] *C.P.R.* *1555–7*, p. 207.   [3] Ibid. *1558–60*, p. 132.
[4] Ibid., p. 381.

Richard Mallory, and Nicholas Bacon,[1] of whom certainly four and perhaps all six were future members of the company, as was probably John Marshe. Such transactions throw some light on the economic position of members and may give some indication of their common interests and activities.

Finally there is the question of friendship, a thing so elusive that it may hardly be worth considering. There were of course well-known friendships between Londoners in this period, of which those between Sir William Cordell and Sir Thomas White and between White and Sir Andrew Judde are examples. Friendships are not easy to discover after the lapse of 400 years, but wills suggest that a good many existed between members of the company. Thus Sir George Barne left £6 13s. 4d. to his 'loving friend' John Southcote,[2] Philip Gunter left a silver cup value £10 to Cecil,[3] Henry Herdson left a gown of 'pewke' to William Garrard and a gown to Ralph Greneway's wife,[4] Sir Roger Martin left £26 13s. 4d. to Anthony Hickman's children,[5] Richard Pointer left a black gown to his friend Robert Wolman and a gold ring to his friend Edmund Roberts,[6] and Anthony Hussey left a gilt pot to the Dean of Canterbury and York which Alderman Chester had given him, a ring value £5 to Chester himself, a ring to Sir William Garrard, and bequests of money for Chester's scholars at Trinity Hall.[7] More interesting are the circles of friendship revealed by bequests of gold rings of remembrance. Thus Humphrey Baskerfeld left rings value 40s. each to a wide circle of friends and relations who included Roger Martin, Edward Jackman, Edmund Stile, Thomas Heton, and John Hare.[8] John Hare left similar rings to Roger Martin, Thomas Gresham, William Hawtrey, Thomas Heton, Francis Barnham, and Edward Jackman.[9] Finally Jackman himself left rings to Lionel Duckett, Roger Martin, John Rivers, Henry Becher, Rowland Heyward, Thomas Lodge, and Richard

[1] Ibid., *1549–51*, p. 202.   [2] P.C.C. 13 Noodes.   [3] P.C.C. 8 Rowe.
[4] P.C.C. 38 More.   [5] P.C.C. 1 Martyn.
[6] P.C.C. 9 Stevenson.   [7] P.C.C. 52 Mellershe.
[8] P.C.C. 9 Stevenson.   [9] P.C.C. 5 Morrison.

Chamberlain's widow.[1] Even if these circles intersected rather than coincided, they suggest a considerable group of members bound together by the real if intangible ties of common friendship.

Members of a trading company had always some common interests arising from the very fact of membership. In the regulated company where, within the company framework, members traded in competition with each other, they had a common interest in defending the company's geographical monopoly of trade and in maintaining regulations designed to limit membership. In the joint-stock company, where the company traded as a body, members had a common interest in the prosperity of that trade upon which the preservation of their capital and the creation of an annual 'increase' depended. Such a common interest demanded the maintenance of monopoly, not because members traded individually within the company's monopoly area, but because the company's profits seemed to depend in part upon the exclusion of interlopers. The absence of competition among the members of the joint-stock company might appear to give them a greater community of interest than was to be found among the competing members of the regulated company. That is possible, but it should be remembered that many members of the Russia Company can have played little active part in its trade and where they did play an active part in trade, it was in other branches where they competed.

The members of the Russia Company were shareholders in it, but it would be anachronistic to endow them with the qualities of the modern holders of ordinary shares, who are often unknown to each other and whose interest in their company, apart from its dividends, is usually as limited as is their knowledge of the business it conducts. The shareholders in the Russia Company were, by modern standards, few in number and they were mainly drawn from the limited geographical area of London. Those facts alone would point to a greater cohesion than is to be found among the shareholders of a modern public company. In

---

[1] P.C.C. 3 Lyon.

addition the members of the company were mainly, though not entirely, drawn from a section of the London population which had certain common interests and activities. No doubt within that section there were wide disparities of wealth and even of social position, but they were hardly wide enough to constitute unbridgeable gaps between members. Finally the members, even if their interest in the Russia Company were limited to that of shareholders, may well have been actively engaged in other branches of foreign trade and may thus have borne the common stamp of ' the great marchaunt man ' whose dealings and virtues were made into a primer ' very preaty for children to rede '.[1] To that side of their activities it is necessary to turn in order to see whether the charter was merely conferring a courtesy title when it described so many of the members as ' merchants of London '.

[1] T. Newbery, *A booke in Englysh metre, of the great Marchaunt man called Dives Pragmaticus, very preaty for children to rede* (1563) ed. P. E. Newbery.

CHAPTER III

TRADING ACTIVITIES

NEARLY three-quarters of the charter members of the Russia Company were described as merchants of London and many of those who were classified by status as knights, esquires, and gentlemen might well have been given the same description. Merchant of London is not however a very informative title, even if it is assumed that it was applied to those whose main interests were in foreign trade, for it tells little of the nature and extent of the trade pursued by members. It is necessary therefore to examine more closely the trading activities of members and to try to discover how far these shareholders in the Russia Company were active merchants and in what branches of trade they were interested.

When the Russia Company received its charter there were already in existence two old established companies to which merchants could belong. Both of these, the Staplers' Company and the Merchant Adventurers' Company, were regulated companies in which members traded individually or in partnerships, providing their own capital and conducting their own businesses subject to the general rules laid down by the company. Though these companies were different in organization from the Russia Company, there was naturally a considerable common membership among the older companies and the new. Of the two older companies, that of the Staplers was already in decline. It had long been concerned almost exclusively with the export of wool and the decline in wool exports linked it with a dying trade. It is true that wool exports showed a temporary increase in the first half of the fifteen-fifties, but in 1560 the Staplers were shipping only about 2000 sacks from London.[1] It would be

[1] E. E. Rich, *The Ordinance Book of the Merchants of the Staple*, pp. 19, 23-4.

rash to assume that the decline in wool exports was the reason why Staplers invested in the Russia Company, but of the Staplers exporting wool from London between Michaelmas 1554 and Michaelmas 1555, at least 7 and possibly 14 became members of the company.[1] In all 13 members of the Russia Company were at one time or another Staplers and another 13 may well have been. Of those members about whom there is no doubt, 3 became mayors of the Staple. Sir Andrew Judde was mayor in 1552 and 1558, Sir William Chester in 1561, and Sir Thomas Offley in 1560, 1564, 1565, and 1569. The last two were concerned in drawing up the Staplers' new Book of Ordinances of 1565.[2]

The decline of the Staplers' was associated with the rise of the Merchant Adventurers' Company. The expanding cloth industry in England consumed the wool which might otherwise have been sent abroad and the cloth made from that wool, insofar as it was exported, was exported largely by the Merchant Adventurers. As cloth accounted for about 80 per cent by value of England's exports in the year ending Michaelmas 1565 [3] and as most cloth was exported through London, a London merchant engaged in the export trade was likely to handle at least some cloth. If he shipped cloth to north-western Europe he would probably, in 1555, send it to Antwerp, the greatest cloth market on the continent, and if he traded with Antwerp he had to belong to the Merchant Adventurers' Company whose members possessed, in theory at least, a monopoly of English trade with that town which constituted their staple. Thus the members of the Merchant Adventurers' Company played a very important part in London's foreign trade, but it is not always possible to be certain who those members were. No complete list of members seems to have survived, for the names given in the Adventurers' charter of 1564 are only a selection. Even so it

---

[1] Exch. K. R. Customs Accounts, 87/7.   [2] Rich, op. cit., p. 105.
[3] Lans. MSS. 10, no. 29. This was not a typical year as the total value of exports was abnormally high, but the evidence suggests that in a more normal year the cloth exports would constitute about 75 per cent of the total.

is possible to discover the names of many Merchant Adventurers at this time and to show that some of them were also members of the Russia Company.

Though attempts to estimate the common membership of these two companies must necessarily be tentative, it would seem that 26 members of the Russia Company were certainly at one time or another also members of the Merchant Adventurers' Company. A further 16 or 17 were probably members of both companies. Few of these men seem to have held the highest office in the Merchant Adventurers' Company. Sir William Dansell was governor in 1551 when he was acting as financial agent for the crown and he continued to hold the governorship when he had been dismissed from his office of agent. Anthony Hussey was governor from 1555 to 1558 and he left £100 Flemish to the company to make a table of remembrance of him.[1] He was probably succeeded by John Marshe who was governor in 1559. Three or four others were assistants in the Merchant Adventurers' Company. They included John Quarles, who left £100 to the company to be used for providing loans for two young men for two years at a time.[2]

It is not certain that mere membership of the Merchant Adventurers' Company necessarily indicated an active trader, but a good many members of the Russia Company were engaged in the export of cloth. Thus between 1547 and 1554 at least 44 and probably as many as 77 future members of the company were exporting cloth.[3] Again a list of London cloth exporters of 1559, which is very incomplete for it covers the export of only 27,174 cloths, includes the names of at least 27 members of the company.[4] This connexion between the members of the company and the cloth trade raises two points of interest. In the first place it suggests that many members of the company were active traders and were in fact Merchant Adventurers. In the second place it may throw some light on a statement which

---

[1] P.C.C. 52 Mellershe.   [2] P.C.C. 3 Langley.
[3] Exch. K.R. Customs Accounts, 87/4, 167/1.
[4] S.P.D. Eliz., vi. no. 52.

the company made in 1600. In explaining its origin the company then declared that ' in the time of King Edward the Sixthe the king and his councell, finding it inconvenient that the utterance of the comodities of England, especiallie clothe, should soe muche depend uppon the Lowe Countries and Spaine and that it should be beneficiall to have a vent some other waies, did encourage his subiectes the merchauntes to adventure for discoverie of new trades northe warde '.[1] A company founded partly to find a new market for cloth might be expected to attract the existing cloth exporters as indeed the Russia Company did.

How far the Russia Company attracted men who traded outside the monopoly areas of the Staplers and the Merchant Adventurers it is difficult to say. The company imported goods similar to those produced in the Baltic countries, but few of the members seem to have been engaged in the Baltic trade. Nor were many members engaged in the Levant trade, which in part consisted of those eastern products the company hoped to tap by a discovery of the north-east passage. Only 3 or 4 members can be shown to have taken part in that trade before its mysterious decline in the late fifteen-fifties. More members were engaged in the trade with France, but it is only possible to identify about a dozen of them. That is certainly, however, an underestimate of their number.[2] The trade with Spain and Portugal seems to have been more important to members of the company. Nineteen can certainly be identified as engaged in it and another 7 or 8 were probably so engaged. Two of these merchants, Edward Castelin and Anthony Hickman, traded with the Canaries where they employed two factors, Edward Kingsmill and Thomas Nicholas. In 1559 Kingsmill was accused of exporting money and of keeping his books in English instead of in Spanish, and

[1] S.P. Foreign Russia, i. f. 133.
[2] Exch. K.R. Customs Accounts, 86/6, which deals with London imports for the year ending Michaelmas 1557 but without giving the places of shipment, shows about 20 members of the company importing goods which almost certainly came from France.

was fined 1000 ducats.   Later both he and Nicholas were charged with religious offences and the latter was imprisoned for about three years.   Though Nicholas claimed that his masters, Castelin and Hickman, lost 14,000 ducats by his imprisonment, they were still trading with Spanish territory in 1564.[1]

It was possibly this trade with Spain, Portugal, and the Canaries which paved the way for that English trade with the west coast of Africa that developed in the middle of the sixteenth century. This development of trade to the south might be expected to attract at least some of the merchants who were pioneering the new trade with Russia.   That indeed was so in the case of the Barbary, Guinea, and to a lesser extent the slaving voyages. Thus the Barbary voyage of 1552 was promoted by a group of men which included three future members of the Russia Company, Sir John York, Sir Thomas Wroth, and William Garrard, as well as a Francis Lambert who was probably the charter member of that name.   Of the 13 merchants who shipped goods for Barbary in the *Grace of God* in 1555, 4 were certainly and 3 more were probably members of the Russia Company.   The early voyages to Guinea were promoted by groups of merchants who were almost all charter members of the Russia Company. Thus of the 5 promoters of the Guinea voyage of 1553, 3 or 4 were later charter members and all 5 of the promoters of the voyage in the following year were probably to become charter members.   The promoters of 1554 included Anthony Hickman and Edward Castelin, who had established their trade with the Canaries by 1555 if not before.   When the ships of the Guinea voyage of 1558 called at the Canaries on the way out they traded there through Edward Kingsmill, Hickman's and Castelin's factor.[2]   The ships included the *Christopher Bennett* which was partly owned by Thomas Bannister, one of the promoters of the voyage and a charter member of the Russia Company.   The *Christopher Bennett*, which was lost on the French coast on the

---

[1] L. de Alberti and A. B. W. Chapman, ' English traders and the Spanish Inquisition in the Canaries ', *T.R.H.S.*, 3rd series, iii. 237–53 ; *C.S.P. For. 1564–5*, p. 19.   [2] Williamson, *Sir John Hawkins*, p. 49.

return voyage, had previously belonged to Geoffrey Vaughan, another charter member.

It has been suggested that the promoters of these Guinea voyages were probably more numerous than 'the published names' imply.[1] That indeed seems to have been the case. Hitherto few names of the promoters of the Guinea voyage of 1558 have been known, but a document of 28 May 1561 shows that 34 merchants were 'owners, laders, and adventurers of the goodd shipps called the *Minion*, the *Christopher*,[2] and the *Tower*[3] of London with the pynnis called the *Unicorne* of the same, and of all and singular the gooddes, wares, and marchaundizes chardged and freighted therein' for the voyage of 1558 'towards the coaste of Giney'. Of these 34 merchants, 22 were probably charter members of the Russia Company.[4]

The Guinea voyages of the early 'sixties, according to the surviving names, were promoted by William Chester, William Garrard, Thomas Lodge, Anthony Hickman, and Edward Castelin, all charter members, with the addition of the Queen, who loaned some of the ships, and of Benjamin Gonson in 1561 and 1564 and William Winter in 1561. These voyages coincided with the beginning of the slave trade between West Africa and the West Indies promoted by syndicates of London merchants who included members of the Russia Company. Thus Lionel Duckett and Thomas Lodge were promoters of

---

[1] Ibid., p. 43.   [2] i.e. the *Christopher Bennett*.
[3] This appears to be a mistake for the *Tiger* (Hakluyt, iv. 111–30).
[4] H.C.A. Libels, 37. no. 247. The 22 were William Chester, William Garrard, Thomas Lodge, Thomas Nicoles the elder, Lionel Duckett, John Broke, draper, Thomas Smith, customer, Sir Andrew Judde, Edward Jackman, Edmund Roberts, Henry Becher, Francis Robinson, Robert Brown, goldsmith, William Merick, Geoffrey Vaughan, Anthony Gamage, Geoffrey Walkeden, Anthony Hickman, Thomas Bannister, Edward Castelin, Miles Mording, and Ralph Greneway. The remaining promoters were John White, James Hawes, John Gresham, Richard Lambert, Richard Pype, Thomas Kightley, William Cooke, James Harvye, Richard Clough, William Allgor (this name is difficult to decipher ; it is possible that it should read Allyn), Thomas Offley (not described as alderman and therefore not the charter member of that name), all merchants of London, and Thomas Kelk, merchant of Bristol.

Hawkins's first slaving voyage of 1562 and Pembroke, Cecil, William Garrard, William Chester, and Edward Castelin were all concerned in the second voyage of 1564, which was said to have made a profit of 60 per cent.[1]   Garrard, Duckett, and Rowland Heyward were among the promoters of the voyage of 1567.   These Guinea and slaving voyages were financed on a joint-stock basis in which the capital and the profits, if any, were distributed at the end of each voyage.   The surviving names of the promoters of these voyages show that a group of the Russian Company members were actively concerned in opening up new trades southwards.

It is necessary to consider how far the charter members were actively concerned in opening up the trade with Russia itself, that is, how far they played an active role in that trade apart from investing their capital in it.   In the absence of the company's own records, which were destroyed in the Great Fire of 1666, the finer details of its organization will probably never be known, but the outline of that organization is reasonably clear.   The company had its headquarters in London where the assembly and the court of assistants met.   The exact functions of the assembly are uncertain, but they included the appointment of the governors, consuls, and assistants, who together constituted the court of assistants.   The court of assistants was the law-making body and it, or a group of its members, determined the trading policy of the company.   The actual conduct of the trade was in the hands of paid employees of the company. In London there was an agent and a secretary and in Russia a chief agent in Moscow, who had general supervision over the trade and over the subordinate agents or factors in other towns.

Such an organization did not allow many of the 201 members of the company to play a very active part in the conduct of the trade unless they were or became governors, consuls, and assistants, or unless they were themselves employed as agents.   No complete records of governors, consuls, and assistants have survived, but at least five charter members became governors after

[1] Williamson, *Sir John Hawkins*, p. 113.

Cabot's death and at least ten, who were not assistants in 1555, later held that position. Some of these men played a considerable role in the company's affairs. Sir George Barne and William Garrard were described as 'the principall doers' in promoting the first voyage of 1553.[1] Barne, who was a consul in the company and 'the cheyff marchand of Muskovea ',[2] died in February 1558, but his eldest son George was later a member and four or five times governor of the company. Garrard, who was a consul in 1555, became governor at least twice. He died in September 1571 but the news of his death took some time to reach Russia for Anthony Jenkinson, who was negotiating with the Tsar for a redress of the company's grievances, was still referring to ' Sir William Garrard and his company ' in the spring of 1572.[3] Rowland Heyward, an assistant in 1555, was subsequently governor five or six times, a position he seems to have held as late as 1587 when Theodor's privileges were granted to ' Sir Rowland Haiward and his societie '.[4] Others too seem to have maintained a long connexion with the company. Burghley, who as Sir William Cecil had been a charter member in 1555, was described forty years later as ' now the most ancient person living of all the said company '.[5] Even this record was broken if Robert Dove, a charter member, was the merchant tailor of that name who was born in 1523, died in 1612 and was apparently a member in 1605.

Some members, who may not have taken much part in the government of the company, were able to play an active role by becoming the company's employees. In the 'sixties and probably in the 'fifties too, the company employed a secretary or clerk called Thomas Nicholes who may have been one of the two charter members of that name. One of those members was described as a goldsmith. Was he the Thomas Nichols, goldsmith, who published a translation of Thucydides from the French version of Claude de Seyssel in 1550? And was the

---

[1] J. Stow, *Annales*, ed. 1631. p. 609. [2] Machyn, p. 166.
[3] Hakluyt, ii. 136–56. [4] Ibid., p. 279.
[5] *H.M.C. Salisbury*, v. 462.

translator also the company secretary ? It is impossible to say, but to make the situation more complicated, the secretary of the Merchant Adventurers' Company at this time was also called Thomas Nicholes. Had the two companies a common secretary ? Perhaps the secretaryship of the Merchant Adventurers involved too much attendance at the staple town on the continent for it to be held in plurality. The London agents of the Russia Company seem rather more identifiable than the elusive secretary. Richard Foulkes, an assistant of 1555, was apparently agent in 1564 when a cargo for Russia was entered in his name by the customs officials, for it was usual for the cargoes to be recorded in the name of the London agent. The following year John Broke was the London agent, a position he held until at least 1569. When he ceased to be agent about 1570 he was said to owe the company £851 1s. 3d. ' for so much redye money and marchandise which he tooke out of their accountes, he being their agent of all their buisnes '.[1]

It is possible that Broke began his service with the company by going out to Vardö as their agent or factor in 1555. Most members of the company were, of course, stay-at-home shareholders, but a few of them did go to Russia either as factors or shipmasters. The three ships which made the first voyage of 1553 carried a large number of merchants,[2] of whom some must have perished when two of the ships were frozen in the ice and all on board died from the cold. Three of the merchants who travelled in the third ship, George Burton, Arthur Edwards, and Thomas Fraunces, appear two years later as charter members. The first voyage was exceptional for the destination was unknown, but on later voyages the ships sometimes carried out factors who were also members of the company. Thus Arthur Edwards went out to Russia again in 1555 and probably stayed there, for he was in the country two years later. After the

---

[1] S.P.D. Eliz., cviii. nos. 62–3.

[2] Hakluyt, i. 244–46 implies that there were 18 merchants on board the three ships, but the account in Cotton MSS., Otho, E VIII, ff. 11–12, does not describe all these men as merchants.

company had opened up trade with Persia through Russia, Edwards was employed as a factor in that trade. In May 1565 he was at Yaroslav getting goods and provisions together for the third Persian voyage, which he accompanied to Shamakhi and Kazbin, but only in a subordinate capacity, for Richard Johnson and Alexander Kitchen were the agents for the voyage. He returned to Russia in 1567, but was back in Persia the following year in charge of the fourth voyage, of which he later gave an account to Richard Willes.[1] Finally Edwards was one of the four agents sent on the sixth and last voyage to Persia in 1579, but he never reached his destination for he was left in charge of part of the goods at Astrakhan where he died in 1580.[2] Before setting out for Persia he had made his will in which he left his 'benefitte or freedome of Muscovia, Media and Persia in the parties beyond the seas' to his cousin John Davenant, the elder, citizen and merchant tailor of London.[3]

Edwards was not the only member of the company employed in the Persian trade. In 1568 Thomas Bannister and Geoffrey Duckett went out to Russia with Thomas Randolph, an ambassador who was to try to get new privileges from the Tsar. Bannister and Duckett were sent out partly as technical experts to assist in the trade negotiations and to put a stop to the private trade conducted by the company's servants and partly to take charge of the fifth Persian voyage. They helped Randolph in the negotiations which resulted in a new grant of privileges, and then left for Persia. Bannister was buying raw silk at Arrash in July 1571 when 'by reason of the unwholesomeness of the aire and corruption of the waters in the hote time of the yeere, he with Lawrence Chapman and some other Englishmen unhappily died'. Duckett remained in Persia until 1573 and later wrote some 'observations' on the customs, religion, and

[1] *D.N.B.*, Richard Willes or Willey (fl. 1558–73). He was not the same man as the Richard Willes or Wilkes who was a charter member of the company.
[2] Hakluyt, i. 308, 389 ; ii. 33–4, 41–53, 108–19, 171–200.
[3] P.C.C. 4 Darcy.

trade of the country.[1]   Duckett was not himself a charter member, but he may have been related to Sir Lionel or to Richard Duckett who were.

While some charter members acted as agents in Russia and Persia, others were concerned with the ships which carried goods between London and St. Nicholas on the White Sea. Cabot's sailing days were over by the time he became governor of the company, but he drew up elaborate ordinances for the conduct of the first voyage of 1553.   Others, who were to become charter members, were more actively engaged in that voyage.   John Buckland was mate of the *Edward Bonaventure* of which Stephen Borough was master.   In the voyage of two years later Buckland was master of the ship, which was wrecked on the return voyage of 1556.   Buckland was one of the survivors of the wreck.   In that he was more fortunate than Richard Chancellor.   Chancellor was pilot general of the fleet and captain of the *Edward Bonaventure* in the voyage of 1553.   He landed at St. Nicholas and travelled to Moscow where he had an interview with the Tsar, of which, and of Russia in general, he wrote an interesting account.[2]   He returned to England the following year and left again for Russia as 'grand pilot' in 1555.   He was returning to England in the *Edward Bonaventure* in company with the first Russian ambassador to this country, when the ship was wrecked on the coast of Scotland in November 1556 and Chancellor was drowned in helping to save the ambassador.   A Nicholas Chancellor, perhaps Richard's son, was later sent as an apprentice to Russia, where he became one of the company's servants.[3]

Stephen Borough, master of the *Edward Bonaventure* in 1553 and a charter member two years later, was long engaged in voyages to Russia as a shipmaster.   Down to at least 1571 he was in charge of ships making the long and hazardous voyage

---

[1] Add. MSS. 35831, ff. 275–8 ; Hakluyt, ii. 85–95, 119–33.   For the identification of Arrash, a town in Transcaucasia, see Morgan and Coote, i. 136, ii. 389.

[2] Hakluyt, i. 254–66.

[3] Ibid., i. 405, ii. 205 ;   Add. MSS. 35831, f. 276.

to and from the White Sea. His son Christopher was one of the company's servants in the Persian voyage of 1579, of which Hakluyt published an account based on Christopher's letters to his uncle, William Borough.[1] William himself made a number of voyages to Russia as a shipmaster and was later a member of the company.[2]

The ships engaged in the Russia trade were sometimes hired by the company from private owners. Thus of the four ships sent to Russia in 1557 at least three belonged to men who were members of the company. The *Primrose* of 240 tons belonged to Andrew Judde, William Chester, Anthony Hickman, and Edward Castelin, the *John Evangelist* to Judde and Chester, and the *Anne* to John Dymocke. The owner of the *Trinity* was given as R.T. Was he Richard Taylor, another member? The whole question of shipownership in this period is obscure, for the history of English merchant shipping has still to be written. It is clear that some members of the Russia Company were owners of ships, apart from those hired to the company in 1557. Thus in 1545 William Bulley was owner of the *Martin Bulley* which was sent out on a privateering expedition financed by Bulley, Sir John Gresham, William More, the captain, and William Hollande, the master of the ship.[3] The following year William Bulley, Anthony Hussey, John Hopkins, and three others were owners of the *White Hind* and a ' calabasse ' which took a French ship as prize. They were bound in recognisance of £1000 to restore 51 bales of cloth from the ship to their rightful owners.[4] Hussey was at that time a judge in the Court of Admiralty.[5] He was also then, or later, a Master in Chancery and chief registrar to the Archbishop of Canterbury.[6] In 1552 Hussey, Bulley, and a Thomas Sullyant were owners of the *Anthony* engaged in bringing sugar from Antwerp, of which four chests were lost through the negligence of the

[1] Hakluyt, ii. 172–201.
[2] Ibid., ii. 133–5, 169 ; Morgan and Coote, ii. 188, 256.
[3] Marsden, i. 139–41.   [4] *A.P.C. 1542–7*, pp. 374, 376, 410.
[5] Marsden, i. lix–lx, 197.   [6] Machyn, p. 380 n.

owners.[1] When he died in 1560 Hussey left £10 and a ring to 'Mr Bulley', who was to clear and reckon all accounts between himself and Hussey for the *Mary Katherine* and for salt lately at Radcliffe. He also left £100 to each of his daughter Ursula's children.[2] She married Benjamin Gonson, Treasurer of the Navy, and their daughter Katherine married Sir John Hawkins. Bulley and Hussey seem to have been joint owners of the *Mary Katherine*,[3] but Bulley is not recorded as owning any ships at his death ; he left however a quay and a wharf called ' Sabbes Key ' in the parish of St. Dunstan in the East to his wife for life with reversion to his four sons.[4]

John Hopkins, part owner of the *White Hind* in 1546, was owner also of a ship trading with Spain some ten years later. According to Hopkins's servant and apprentice, Henry Lumnour, a native of Sharrington in Norfolk, the freighters of the ship, Edward Jackman and company, failed to load the 80 tons of cargo provided for in the charter party.[5] About the same time Hopkins owned a ship carrying beer and ox horns to Antwerp. If the water did not get into the wine, the ox horns seem to have got too near to the beer. On the ship's arrival at Antwerp an elaborate beer tasting took place in which the crew participated. Richard Byrde, mariner, declared that ' some barrells of the same bere was worser then some other barrells in drynckyng to this deponent's taste ', but William Harrison, a Yorkshireman who should have known what he was talking about, thought the beer ' drancke verye tastelye '.[6]

The two Canary merchants, Hickman and Castelin, sold a ship, the *Great Christopher* of 800 tons, to the Queen in 1560.[7] They do not however seem to have owned any of the ships engaged in their Guinea ventures, but William Chester and

---

[1] Marsden, ii. 80–1.   [2] P.C.C. 52 Mellershe.

[3] H.C.A. Examinations, 11 (25 April 1556).

[4] P.C.C. 38 Pyckering. It does not seem possible to identify this quay, but as Stow pointed out (i. 135) the quays in that parish ' commonly beare the names of their owners, and are therefore changeable '.

[5] H.C.A. Examinations, 10 (3 Nov. 1555).   [6] Ibid. (27 Nov. 1555).

[7] M. Oppenheim, *History of the administration of the royal navy*, pp. 122–3.

William Garrard owned a ship captured by the Portuguese in the Elmina region in 1565 and another taken while watering in the Azores the following year. Garrard was also part owner of the *Primrose*, which was engaged in the Guinea voyage of 1553. Henry Fallowfield, another charter member, had his ship seized by the Spaniards when it was driven into Bilbao by a storm in September 1565. The pretext for the seizure was that the ship had been engaged in piracy the year before, when, according to Fallowfield, it was safely in harbour at Portsmouth.[1] Perhaps Fallowfield got his ship back, for in 1566 he left his ' shippe with all the goods in the same shippe ' to his wife and his son.[2] The ship was probably the *Hart*, for after Fallowfield's death his widow brought an action against George Thornton, master of the *Hart*, for taking up money on bills of exchange in Spain which he said was necessary for repairs to the ship, but for which Fallowfield had refused to accept responsibility.[3] As Fallowfield left £10 to his sister Agnes Thornton, it is probable that the master of his ship was related to him.

Finally two charter members of the Russia Company seem to have been shipowners on a fairly large scale. William Bond was part owner of the *Pelican*, which was seized in 1572 by French pirates who murdered the crew and took goods worth £4000 from the ship.[4] This was clearly not the only ship in which Bond was interested. When he died in 1576 he left gold rings value 40s. each to the masters of his five ships.[5] Perhaps it was not a very ample reward for running the risk of being murdered by French pirates. Geoffrey Vaughan, owner of the *Christopher Bennett* in 1553, bought the *Hart* of Bristol for £300 from William Winter in the same year.[6] Two years later he shared with George Thornton the ownership of

---

[1] Lans. MSS. 98, no. 11 ; R. Ascham, *Works*, ed. J. A. Giles, ii. 104–6, 122–3.
[2] P.C.C. 17 Crymes.
[3] H.C.A. Examinations, 16 (18 Oct. 1566).
[4] Oppenheim, *Administration of the royal navy*, pp. 179–80.
[5] P.C.C. 26 Carew.
[6] H.C.A. Examinations, 9 (9 June 1554).

a ship trading with Spain, which the freighters, who included Thomas Chamber, failed to load in accordance with the charter party and had therefore to pay compensation for ' dead freight '.[1] This ship may have been the *Mary Fortune*, which Vaughan owned or partly owned and which traded with Spain.[2]   In the fifteen-sixties Vaughan was part owner of another ship, the *Marmoset*, which also traded with Spain.[3]   Thus Bond and Vaughan were fairly large shipowners, but neither could compare with their contemporary, Olyff Burr, ' the coppersmith ', whose ships are almost as ubiquitous in the records as they must have been on the seas.

Shipowning carried many risks, but these could be lessened by the common practice of owning parts in a number of ships and by insurance.   Thus members of the Russia Company sometimes owned a ship and sometimes a part of a ship.   How far such ships were covered by insurance it is impossible to say, for the whole subject of marine insurance in this period awaits exploration.   It is clear that members of the company were sometimes engaged in insurance business, either of ships or of their cargoes.   Thus in 1548 a group of underwriters insured an Italian ship, the *Santa Maria*, which carried cloth from Southampton to Messina.   The group included Blase Saunders, Thomas Castell, Thomas Chamber, William Merick, and John Dymocke, all of whom seem later to have become charter members.[4]   Castell and Chamber with Robert Dove and others were underwriters of a ship trading between Spain and Antwerp in 1559.[5]   Six years later Dove was concerned in the insurance of the *St. John Baptist* on a voyage from Leghorn to Cadiz during which the ship sank.[6]   Finally in 1564 Richard Springham, defendant in a High Court of Admiralty case, could refer to ' William Meredithe of whose company of assurance this respondent is one '.   Springham explained that it was the custom

---

[1] H.C.A. Examinations, 10 (2 Sept. 1555), 11 (3 Jan. 1556) ; Marsden, ii. 97–8.
[2] H.C.A. Examinations, 14 (23 Oct. 1561).   [3] Ibid., 15 (11 May 1566).
[4] Marsden, ii. 45–6.   [5] Ibid., ii. 51.   [6] Ibid., ii. 132.

of Lombard Street ' that if it dothe not appeare of any right, title or interest that the partie that maketh the assurance or causeth himself to be assured upon the shipp, apparell, freight or other goods, wares or marchaundices that is so assured, that then the assurers of the same ar not bownde to pay annye sum by them assured '. According to Springham the plaintiff had no title, right or interest in the ship and so he, Springham, refused to pay him ' the som by the saide Meredithe assured '. The plaintiff was Robert Ridolfi, banker and plotter.[1] Such examples tell little but they suggest yet another aspect of foreign trade in which members of the company were interested.

An examination of the trading activities of members of the company leads to the conclusion that many of those members were actively engaged in foreign trade. If only those members who can be identified with certainty are considered, then about half of them can be shown to have been engaged in foreign trade between 1547 and 1559.[2] This is not an unimpressive proportion considering the nature of the evidence, for the Port Books do not begin until 1565 and the customs accounts are not easy to use for this type of detailed investigation. To go further than this, to calculate the foreign trade of individual merchants quantitatively, presents insuperable difficulties. After 1565 the Port Books might be used with caution for this purpose, but the Elizabethan Port Books for London are too few to give any complete picture of a merchant's activities. Nor do private business records appear to have survived for this period.[3] It is only possible therefore to offer some tentative reflections on the scope and organization of the trade pursued by individual members of the company.

The bigger merchants do not seem to have specialized in one branch of trade exclusively. In addition to their interest in the Russia Company, they traded with many countries, often

[1] H.C.A. Examinations, 15 (25 June 1564).

[2] This calculation is based on the evidence in Exch. K.R. Customs Accounts, 86/2, 6; 87/4; 90/11; 167/1; S.P.D. Eliz., vi. no. 52.

[3] Where, for example, is George Stoddard's ' ancient account-book ' which Hall used in his *Society in the Elizabethan Age* ?

apparently simultaneously. Thus Sir William Chester exported wool to Calais and cloth, which almost certainly went to Antwerp. He traded with France, Barbary, and the Guinea coast. Sir William Garrard exported cloth to the continent and imported sugar from Barbary. He was engaged in the Guinea and the slave trade. Sir Thomas Lodge exported wool to Calais and to foreign parts beyond the Straits. He exported cloth, presumably to Antwerp, and imported 'sugar and spice and all that's nice,' presumably from the same place. He helped to bring gold and ivory from Africa and to send the Africans as slaves to the New World. Perhaps it was all to no purpose, for ' this Sir T. Lodge braky and professe to be banqwerooute in his maioralitie to the grete slandar of the citie '.[1] Did his contemporaries ascribe his failure, which may have been more apparent than real, to the fact that he was a pioneer in other directions than trade for he ' ware a beard, and was the fyrst that (beynge Mayr of London) ever ware eny, the whiche was thowght to mayny people very straynge to leve the cumly aunsyent custom of shavynge theyr beards ' ? However he ' ware the comly auncient bonet with iiij cornars ', whereas his successor, Sir John White ' ware bothe a longe beard and allso a rownd cape, that wayed not iiij ouncis, whiche semyd to all men, in consyderation of the auncient bonyt, to be very uncomly '.[2]

Trade with a variety of places led to trade in a variety of products, though a merchant who dealt only with Antwerp could find at that entrepôt all types of European and eastern commodities. The evidence, which is admittedly very imperfect, suggests little specialization by product. William Bond exported cloth, including cottons, and imported wine ; Anthony Gamage exported cottons, lead, and wax, and imported canvas ; Richard Patrickes exported cottons and wax and imported onions and probably herrings. The list could be multiplied, but Edward Jackman must serve as the last example of this versatility. Jack-

[1] J. Gairdner, *Three fifteenth-century chronicles*, Camden Society, N.S., xxviii. 127–8.   [2] Ibid.

man exported lead, saffron, and cloth, the cloth going to Antwerp and Barbary. He imported hops and rape oil from Antwerp and sugar from Barbary. It would be wrong to assume that this interest in many products meant that the trade in any one of them was necessarily small. Thus in the year ending Michaelmas 1568 Jackman imported from Barbary 480 cwt. of sugar, a little over 11 tons of unrefined sugar called panele, and 'j chest ostridge fethers '. These goods were officially valued at £1794. In partnership with Francis Bowyer, he imported a further 132 cwt. of sugar.[1]

Trade of this magnitude, often carried on with more than one country, must have involved a considerable organization and staff. Little is known, and may ever be known, of that organization. Merchants learned their trade through apprenticeship, sometimes, as in the case of Thomas Gresham, who was apprenticed to his uncle, Sir John Gresham, even when they could have gained their freedom of a company by patrimony. No doubt it helped for the former apprentice to marry his master's daughter in the traditional manner, as Thomas Offley married Joan, the daughter of his master John Nicholls. In this case the position was consolidated by Thomas's sister Margaret marrying Nicholls himself.[2] When he died Offley left his apprentice, Henry Warde, £10 and a gown.[3] Masters sometimes helped their former apprentices where there was no tie by marriage. Thus Thomas White received £100 under the will of his late master, Hugh Acton. Once out of their apprenticeship and established in trade, the merchants began themselves to take apprentices, whose numbers may be some indication of the scale of business on which their masters were operating. Thus William Chester, who had become free of the Drapers Company by patrimony in 1529, apparently enrolled no fewer than three apprentices in the single year ending August 1553.[4] Anthony Gamage, in his will dated 15 December 1571,

---

[1] Exch. K.R. Port Books, 4/2.
[2] G. C. Bower, ' A manuscript relating to the family of Offley ', *Genealogist*, N.S. xix. 1–11. [3] P.C.C. 39 Tirwhite. [4] Johnson, ii. 398–9.

left bequests ranging from £10 to £3 to each of his six apprentices, as well as £10 to a former apprentice, Thomas Brade of Walsingham. Two of these apprentices, Peter Johnson and James Lorde, were to have the use for four years of £100, part of the £400 which Gamage left to the Ironmongers Company.[1] Edward Jackman left £6 13s. 4d. to each of his four apprentices and made one of them, Oliver Stile, an overseer of his will.[2] Oliver later became a trader to France, Spain, Barbary, and the Levant, as did his brother Nicholas Stile,[3] who had been apprenticed to Jackman's brother-in-law, Richard Lambert, and to whom Jackman left £3 6s. 8d.[4] Sir Roger Martin was more generous. He left £20 to one of his apprentices and £10 to each of the other two.[5] Perhaps the most curious of these bequests was that of Sir Thomas White. When he made his will on 8 November 1566, White had at least three apprentices. To two of them he left £7 and £4 respectively and to the third, Gilbert Moxsey, he left £20, a loan of £100 to be repaid in instalments of £10 p.a., and his 'freedom of Moscovia'. If Moxsey refused the freedom, then it was to go to any other of White's apprentices who would accept it. It is not certain that any of them accepted this unusual offer.[6]

Bequests to apprentices were not always entirely altruistic, for the apprentice in the last years of his service may well have known a good deal about his master's business. Thus Humphrey Baskerfeld left the large sum of £66 13s. 4d. to his apprentice, Richard Cupper, but only on condition that Cupper made a just account of all goods, money, and debts in his charge. Baskerfeld also left £50 to his apprentice, Hugh Baskerfeld. Again it was a large sum, but Hugh was presumably a relative.[7] In some cases apprentices could acquire a knowledge of their masters' business by acting as their factors. Thus in 1555 Thomas

---

[1] P.C.C. 32 Bakon.   [2] P.C.C. 3 Lyon.

[3] *C.S.P.D. 1591-4*, p. 58 ; S.P.D. Eliz., ccliii. no. 28. Oliver and Nicholas Stile were sons of Humphrey Stile, cousin of Edmund Stile, the charter member (P.C.C. 7 Stevenson).

[4] P.C.C. 3 Lyon.   [5] P.C.C. 1 Martyn.

[6] P.C.C. 36 Stonarde.   [7] P.C.C. 9 Stevenson.

Odell and George Whitney explained that they had been sent
to Spain seven years before as servants and apprentices of Henry
Richards and had there acted as his factors in the sale of his
cloth.[1] Similarly Thomas Castell took Henry Clough as his
apprentice in 1552–3 and some five years later sent him to
Spain as his factor. Unfortunately Clough was captured on
the way by the French. He was ransomed by Mighel Darches,
but the cost of his ransom and of bringing him from Le Havre
was said to amount to £150, which neither Castell nor his
partner, Thomas Chamber, was willing to pay.[2] The employment of apprentices as factors meant that the latter were often
very young men. In 1564 John White, aged 32, said that he
had been John Broke's factor for 13 or 14 years. It is not however certain that White had been Broke's apprentice.[3]

Apprentices no doubt sometimes remained in their masters'
employment when their term of apprenticeship was over. This
is rather implied in the bequests made by Henry Becher. In
his will dated 19 June 1568 Becher left £20 to his two employees
who had the chief charge of his books of account in London
and Antwerp and who were to give a true account of his goods
and debts. He also left £6 13s. 4d. to his apprentice, Thomas
Webbe. In a codicil dated 8 December 1570, Webbe was
described as late apprentice and was left a further £5 in return
for giving the executors a just account of the goods and debts.
As James Escott was described in the codicil as being in charge
of the books in London, it rather looks as if Webbe may have
become the Antwerp bookkeeper.[4] The faithful servant must
have been especially important when the merchant died childless
or with only young children. The will of William Dawkes,
who died in August 1555, shows the sort of arrangement that
could be made. Dawkes had two daughters, Elizabeth and
Mary, both unmarried, to whom he left a third of his personal
estate. The use of this third he granted to his brother Richard,

[1] H.C.A. Examinations, 9 (12 Jan. 1555).
[2] Ibid., 13 (13 Feb. 1561), 14 (7 and 9 June 1561) ; Johnson, ii. 398.
[3] H.C.A. Examinations, 15 (2 Oct. 1564).   [4] P.C.C. 10 Holney.

to whom he also left £100 and a bill of exchange of an Antwerp
merchant value £129, and to Richard Blackston, his Antwerp
factor, to whom he also left £40 in return for a true account
of his goods.   The two legatees were only to have the use of
the girls' portions if they occupied their stocks jointly for four
years as co-partners in the trade of merchandise as other merchants
had done in the like trade.   The wording of the will rather
suggests that William and Richard Dawkes had been in partnership and that Richard Blackston had been their apprentice and
factor and was now to take the deceased brother's place as
partner, using half the girls' portions as his capital.[1]

The transition from factor to merchant was probably common.
Edmund Ansell appears as Henry Herdson's factor in Spain in
1541 and was later trading on his own account.   The same is
true of Thomas Castell who was Henry Richards's factor in
Spain in 1544.   Similarly the combination of factor and merchant
was probably also common, for others besides John Sanderson
must have played 'the gentilman, agent, and merchaunt' in
places other than the Levant.[2]   Trading through factors resident
in foreign parts was normal enough, but it is difficult to tell
how many factors merchants employed and how often men
acted as factors for a number of merchants.   The size of his
staff naturally depended on the scale of the merchant's operations,
but in an age when many household and personal servants were
men and boys it is not easy to distinguish the clerks of the
counting house from the servants of the kitchen and stable.
Thus William Bond left £40 to each of nine named servants,
all of them male, and £6 13s. 4d. to each of six other servants.
As he left separate bequests to his maid servants, it seems reasonable to suppose that at least the nine recipients of £40 apiece
were employees in his business, which may also be some indication of the size of that business.[3]

Whether any of Bond's legatees were his factors abroad is not

[1] P.C.C. F 31 More.
[2] *The travels of John Sanderson*, ed. Sir William Foster, p. 17.
[3] P.C.C. 26 Carew.

known, but bequests to such factors do occur. Sir Roger Martin left 100 marks to his servant William Rawlyns, mercer, trusting that he would be as faithful and true to his, Martin's, wife and children as he had been to Martin himself. Martin also left £5 to Roger Rawlyns, his godson, and £5 to Susan Rawlyns, who may have been William's children, and £20 to James Elwike, his servant.[1] William Rawlyns and James Elwike were Martin's factors 'or doers' at Hamburg. They had, like Elizabethan secretaries of state, equal powers 'for that when one was not in the way the other supplied his place'. Thus in 1570 they bought at Hamburg 58 'papers of silk of Verona' for Martin which they packed in a barrel. Elwike then covenanted and agreed with Harman Felter for the carriage of the silk in Felter's boat, the *Jonas*, and saw it put on board. Rawlyns was however informed of this 'for that upon the ladinge thereof the said James Elwike made hym pryvey thereunto as ther order was to make eache other pryvey of all ther doings towchinge the sayde Sir Roger Martyn's affaires and business'. When the *Jonas* arrived at London it was met by Samuel Knowles, Martin's son-in-law, who received the silk at Cox quay. Knowles found however that the barrel was loose at one end and appeared to contain only 51 papers of silk. The barrel was removed to Martin's house in Soper Lane where his sons, Edmund and Humphrey, saw it opened and bore witness to the missing 7 papers. Rawlyns, who was aged 50, testified that the barrel had been duly packed with 58 papers of silk. Such cases were not uncommon, but Martin *v.* Felter shows how two factors could work in double harness in a single port when the merchant's business was large enough to warrant such an arrangement.[2]

Bequests to factors with the request that the legatee should assist in settling up his master's business or help his master's widow, were not uncommon. Sir George Barne left £40 to his servant George Lodge, who was to gather up his, Barne's, goods in Spain.[3] Some years before Barne had employed his

[1] P.C.C. 1 Martyn. [2] H.C.A. Examinations, 18 (25 and 29 Nov. 1570).
[3] P.C.C. 13 Noodes.

own son Philip as his factor in Spain, but Philip may have died in the interval for he is not mentioned in Barne's will. Ralph Greneway also left £40 to his servant in Spain, Richard Soday, who was also his brother-in-law.[1] The employment of relatives in some capacity or other seems to have been not unusual, if identity of surnames can be taken as a sign of kinship. Greneway also left £80 to his servant, John Greneway, who may have been his nephew and was certainly only a boy for he was to be bound apprentice to William Allen, leather-seller, for eight years and the money was to be paid at the end of his service.[2] Similarly John Quarles left £20 to his servant Francis Quarles,[3] and Henry Flammacke left the same amount to John Flammacke, his servant.[4]

When the merchant died in foreign parts and had no factor or relative to wind up his business, difficulties could occur. Thus Philip Kever, who died in Cadiz, left 6 ducats to the poor of that city and some fardels of linen cloth, which were to be sold and after payment of his debts the money from the sale was to go to his wife and children. Kever appointed Thomas Thompson, an English merchant in Cadiz who had previously been his apprentice and servant, as his executor to sell the cloth, pay his debts, and remit the residue to his legatees. According to Kever's widow, Alice, her husband had left goods worth £2320, including ·four ' balles of golde ', which Kever was on the point of bringing to England just before his death, but which he dare not avow as their export would have been illegal. Thompson denied the existence of the gold balls and maintained that Kever's debts exceeded the value of his goods, though in fact Alice seems to have received goods value £600 from her husband's estate. It is not clear how the case ended, but it shows the difficulty a widow might have in winding up her husband's business abroad, a difficulty which might not arise where there was a faithful factor.[5]

Some of the men employed by merchants may not have been

---

[1] P.C.C. F 30 Noodes.   [2] Ibid.   [3] P.C.C. 3 Langley.   [4] P.C.C. 3 Loftes.
[5] P.C.C. 31 More ; Chancery Proceedings, second series, 106. nos. 91, 97.

household servants or factors or clerks in the export and import branch of the business, but assistants in retail trade. Though contemporaries tended to draw a distinction between the merchant and the retailer, even in London the two functions must sometimes have been combined. Retail trade is a more elusive subject than foreign trade for there was no reason why even customs officials should be interested in it.[1] Hence it is almost impossible to say whether the members of the Russia Company, who were or were not actively engaged in foreign trade, were retailers. Some of them apparently were. Robert Dawbeney, merchant tailor, had his shop in Watling Street, Aldermary, where the drapers plied their trade.[2] Robert Downe, ironmonger, had two shops in St. Mary Colechurch.[3] Anthony Gamage was a retailer of linen cloth.[4] Henry Becher, ' myllener ', supplied ' fethers whight and black ', gold sarcenet, and ' Cullen sylver ' and ' Cullen gowlde ' for the court revels, as perhaps did Richard Mallory.[5] Philip Gunter, the young man from Monmouthshire who became ' skinner, alias citizen and upholster of London ', was not even content with the London market. In 1554 the Oxford city council agreed that Philip Gunter, ' bedder ', should ' sell upholsters wares wythyn the lybertyes of thys cytye untyll the feast of Pentycost for the som of £3 except he take a stondyng yn the fayer at the fayer tyme '. Perhaps he beat the council down, for he seems only to have paid £2.[6] Later Gunter had distinguished customers. He supplied bells for ' maskinge apparrell ' and buckram, both for court

---

[1] No doubt the inaccessible inventories of Somerset House and the uncalendared records of the law courts contain information on retail trade, but whether the results of a study of these sources would justify the labour involved is uncertain. The inventory of a London grocer, dated 1601, which is printed in *Transactions of the Lancashire and Cheshire Antiquarian Society*, xxi (1903), shows that this type of record contains interesting and valuable information.

[2] P.C.C. 57 Noodes ; Stow, i. 81.

[3] P.C.C. F 2 Wrastley.　　　　　[4] *C.S.P.D. 1547–80*, p. 620.

[5] A. Feuillerat, *Documents relating to the revels at Court in the time of King Edward VI and Queen Mary*, pp. 135, 256 ; idem, *Documents relating to the office of the revels in the time of Queen Elizabeth*, pp. 82, 87, 93, 99.

[6] W. H. Turner, *Selections from the records of the city of Oxford*, pp. 218, 220.

entertainments,[1] and tapestry and bedding to Sir Henry Sidney for Durham Place and Penshurst.[2] Others doubtless engaged in humbler retail transactions which have left no trace.

The members of the Russia Company were thus, so far as can be ascertained, not only shareholders in the company, but often merchants engaged in many branches of foreign trade and dealers in many types of commodities. In addition some were interested in industrial enterprises. About a dozen of them seem to have been members of the Mines Royal or the Mineral and Battery Works. Sir Henry Sidney and Edmund Roberts were partners in steel works in Kent and iron works in Glamorgan. Sir Thomas Gresham had an iron furnace in Sussex and William Humfrey claimed to have invented a furnace and a sieve for use in lead smelting. Sir William Chester was one of the pioneers of sugar refining in England. The greatest industry of all, cloth making, does not seem to have attracted members, though Sir Thomas White may have made cloth as well as traded in it. He certainly had a stock of cloth at his death for he willed that his late servant, Stephen Frenche, should have £200 worth of that cloth, paying for it in instalments of £15 p.a.[3] There is no evidence however that White had made this cloth. The bequests to clothiers made by Francis Barnham [4] and Humphrey Baskerfeld [5] suggest the normal practice of the London merchant of buying his cloth in the provinces.

These industrial interests show that the members of the Russia Company displayed a certain variety in their economic activities, though naturally their concern with trade was predominant. It remains to consider what sort of a success in a worldly sense they made of their careers in a society which had not yet come to regard worldly success as necessarily a sign of grace.

[1] Feuillerat, *Documents relating to the office of the revels in the time of Queen Elizabeth*, pp. 83, 138, 158, 174, 184.

[2] *H.M.C. Lord de L'Isle and Dudley*, i. 259, 427.

[3] P.C.C. 36 Stonarde.   [4] P.C.C. 10 Carew.   [5] P.C.C. 9 Stevenson.

CHAPTER IV

WEALTH

THE members of the Russia Company, like the society in which they lived, displayed great inequalities in the distribution of wealth. They included men who were or became very rich and men who were and remained so modest in fortune that sometimes little or nothing can be learned of them. At one extreme was Cecil, who as lord Burghley owned so many manors and so many thousands of ounces of plate, who willed that his funeral should not cost more than £1000 and that his de Vere granddaughters should have dowries of £4000 apiece if they married earls or the heirs apparent of earls.[1] At the other extreme was Edmund Roberts, merchant and industrialist, who died bankrupt. Between these extremes lay the majority of members and it is best to try to concentrate on them, ignoring those whose wealth was so great and whose standard of living so prominent that they are well known and those whose resources were apparently so modest and whose way of life was apparently so humble that they have left little trace behind them. If such a concentration distorts the picture, it can only be pleaded that the sources in part demand it.

There are many ways of trying to assess a man's wealth in the sixteenth century. His house and his servants, his ownership of land and of other property, his bequests to his family and to charity, all reveal something of his economic position. No doubt the picture can rarely be complete even in the case of an individual and still less so in the case of a group, but it is nevertheless worth drawing.

The more successful merchants had a house in London and a house in the country as well, to which no doubt they went for sport and to avoid the plague. Thus Sir John Branche had

[1] P.C.C. 91 Lewyn.

a house in the city and Garnish Hall in Essex.[1] Sir Rowland
Heyward had a great house in London which had formerly been
the hospital or priory of Elsing Spittal, and a country house at
Hackney where Elizabeth visited him in 1587. David Woodroff
also maintained two houses, the contents of which he left to his
widow. His London house was 'The Greene Gate', a 'fayre
house of olde time',[2] and at St. Albans he occupied a house
which was not apparently the 'Flower de Luce' which he had
bought there in 1556.[3]

Others maintained only a London house, but that befitted
the owner's wealth and position. William Bond had Crosby
Place, a 'great house . . . , verie large and beautifull', to which
he added 'a turret on the top thereof' and which was later
used to house ambassadors.[4] It was not the only merchant's
house fit for an ambassador. In 1557 Osep Napea, the Russian
ambassador, lodged in John Dymocke's house in Fenchurch
Street.[5] Ten years later 'one ambasador from the Emperowr
and one othar from the Lady Regent of Flaundars' were 'con-
vayde to Master Dymoks place in Fanchurche Strete and ther
lodgyd'.[6] Others, who escaped the doubtful pleasure of lodging
ambassadors, lived in houses which sound as if they would have
been suitable for that purpose. Philip Gunter lived in 'one
great house', the Sarazens Head,[7] in Cornhill, where he carried
on his business. Henry Becher had his mansion in the parish
of St. Christopher by the Stocks on the back of which he built
'a great chamber', which his widow was to occupy.[8] Richard
Chamberlain built himself a mansion in Old Jewry on a site
leased from his company, the Ironmongers.[9] It would be
rash to conclude that these were typical dwellings of London

---

[1] P.C.C. 55 Rutland. [2] Stow, i. 152.
[3] P.C.C. 21 Chayre ; *C.P.R. 1555–7*, pp. 345–6.
[4] Stow, i. 172–3, ii. 299–300 ; Strype, i. bk ii. 105–6. For the furniture
needed for Crosby Place, see the inventory of a former owner (*Inq. p.m. Lond.*,
i. 114–15).
[5] Machyn, pp. 127, 130 ; Hakluyt, i. 367.
[6] Gairdner, *Three fifteenth-century chronicles*, p. 142.
[7] Stow, i. 199, ii. 307. [8] P.C.C. 10 Holney. [9] Nicholl, p. 546.

merchants, but even a much less prosperous man like Thomas Bannister had his ' mansion ' and in addition leased a garden near the church of St. Mary Axe,[1] which may have reminded him of the rose gardens of Persia.

Such houses must have required a considerable staff of servants, but the domestic economy of the middle-class household is little known in comparison with the elaborate domestic arrangements of the nobility. It may be some indication of the size of those staffs that when Sir Roger Martin left a year's wages to his servants, he earmarked £40 for that purpose. In addition he left £6 13s. 4d. to Richard Lowmas, his serving man, and £2 to Joan Clerke, who nursed his daughter Anne.[2] Such bequests to nurses were not unusual.[3] Henry Becher left £1 to his daughter Dorothy's nurse, £2 to the nurse of his sons, Henry and Edward, and £1 to Nurse Fuller's wife. He also left £5 to his cook, John Harte, which was to be paid at the end of Harte's apprenticeship.[4] Male nurses were rarer than male domestic servants, but the evidence of wills rather suggests that the female domestic servant played a greater role in the merchant's household than she did in the household of the queen or the noble. Probably the proportion of female to male servants increased as the wealth and social standing of the master and mistress decreased. Though it is difficult to estimate the number of domestic servants kept by merchants, it is clear that individual servants were highly esteemed. William Bond left £100 to ' Besse, my maid ' to be paid on her marriage, and £6 13s. 4d. to each of his other maids.[5] John Quarles had at least three maid servants, to two of whom he left £13 6s. 8d. each and to one £5. He also left £2 each to Mother Holmes and Mother Agnes.[6] Sir John Branche left £50 to Ellen Spicer, his servant,[7] and Thomas Bannister left £5 to his maid, Katherine Spicer.[8]

---

[1] P.C.C. 1 Carew.   [2] P.C.C. 1 Martyn.

[3] Sir Richard Sackville's bequests to his five physicians (P.C.C. 14 Crymes) suggest hypochondria.

[4] P.C.C. 10 Holney.   [5] P.C.C. 26 Carew.   [6] P.C.C. 3 Langley.

[7] P.C.C. 55 Rutland.   [8] P.C.C. 1 Carew.

Perhaps the Spicers were related and came from one of those families, now almost extinct, in which there was a tradition of going into service.

The faithful servant might get his reward, but he must not take liberties. When Sir Lionel Duckett made his will on 3 September 1585 he left a third of his personal estate to his wife, a third to his only son, Thomas, and a third in various bequests with residue to his wife and son. Among the bequests was one of £20 to his servant Thomas Nelson. In a codicil of 9 July 1587 Duckett sadly explained that his son had married Margaret Nelson, without his consent and against his express command. The residue of the third portion was therefore to go wholly to his, Duckett's, wife, who had taken great pains with and care of him during his long sickness. His London house, which had originally been left to his widow for life only, had been sold and the purchase money was to go to her absolutely. Moreover Thomas Nelson had not dealt well with Duckett over the marriage of Duckett's son to Nelson's kinswoman, and was therefore to lose his legacy of £20. On the other hand, Henry Jones, who had taken great pains during Duckett's sickness, was to have £30 instead of £20, Alice Jones was to have £6 13s. 4d. for the same reason, and Joan Moody, servant and kinswoman, was to have £50 instead of £30. Thus were the righteous rewarded and the presumptuous cast down, but Thomas Duckett was far from being cut off with a shilling for his *mésalliance*, for he still had a third of the personal estate and a share with his mother in the lands.[1]

The houses in which they lived often constituted only a small part of the property owned by members of the company. The extent and value of that property naturally varied a great deal between individuals. It is not necessary to linger over the great landed possessions of Burghley or Sir Nicholas Bacon or Sir William Petre, who had nearly two dozen manors in half a dozen counties. They were exceptional, but the desire for land and houses was common among men of lesser fortune, who

[1] P.C.C. 9 Rutland.

wanted to invest the profits of their trade. The dissolution of the monasteries and the chantries had no doubt increased opportunities for such investment and it is noticeable how many of the property transactions of merchants involved former monastic and chantry lands and houses, not only in the countryside but in the towns as well. Members of the company engaged in many such transactions, which it would be tedious to pursue through the patent rolls and the feet of fines, especially as, at this distance of time, some of them appear as interminable and unintelligible as children's play. Such detailed work requires to be done, but in a general study it is better to concentrate on the final result, rather than the intermediate stages, and try to see what property these London merchants had accumulated by the end of their careers.

The more successful merchants sometimes accumulated large landed estates often dispersed over a number of counties. Thus Henry Becher had property in Somerset, Gloucestershire, Wiltshire, Devon, Surrey, Lincolnshire, Sussex, and Kent, as well as in London. All this was worth, according to the *inquisition post mortem*, £151 16s. 8d. p.a.[1] Sir Rowland Heyward died a great landowner with much London property and some 18 manors, chiefly in Shropshire and Staffordshire, though some of his land was in Buckinghamshire, Bedfordshire, Wiltshire, and Montgomeryshire.[2] Sir William Garrard left lands in Kent, Surrey, and Buckinghamshire,[3] and Francis Barnham had property in Surrey, Essex, and Wales as well as in London.[4] Henry Brunker left manors held in fee simple to the value of £240 2s. 10d. p.a.[5] Not all were so broad-acred as this. At the other extreme of landownership was William Dawkes with a house and some pastures in Worcestershire.[6] That did not necessarily mean that Dawkes was a poor man, for many merchants preferred to invest in urban rather than rural property or preferred other types of investment to real estate.

[1] *Inq. p.m. Lond.*, ii. 150–3. [2] Ibid., iii. 202–10.
[3] P.C.C. 3 Daper. [4] P.C.C. 4 Carew.
[5] P.C.C. 15 Babington. [6] P.C.C. 31 More.

The ownership of urban property by members seems to have been more widespread than the ownership of rural property. Among a group of London merchants that might be expected. The richer men, as Barnham, Becher, and Heyward, owned both, but some of the well-to-do merchants do not seem to have invested in country property at all. Thus Robert Downe, apparently the father of the charter member, left property which, according to the *inquisition post mortem*, was worth £74 13*s*. 4*d*. p.a. This was entirely in London and comprised some 27 messuages, 23 cottages, 30 shops, 10 cellars, and 6 gardens.[1] Sir Thomas White's extensive property of some 60 messuages, tenements, and shops was also in London.[2] William Bond held little property for so wealthy a man, but what he had consisted of London houses.[3] The same seems true of Sir Christopher Draper,[4] Anthony Gamage,[5] and Philip Gunter,[6] who all held little property wholly in London. The less wealthy seem often to have owned the houses they lived in, as did Thomas Bannister, Alexander Carleill, Blase Saunders, and Robert Dawbeney.[7]

Houses in the tenure of their owners eased the problem of providing for the widow, to whom such houses were often left for life. Thus Alexander Carleill left his house in St. Michael Paternoster to his wife Alice for life [8] and Robert Dawbeney left his house, shop, solars, and cellars in Aldermary to his wife Elizabeth for life.[9] Henry Becher, while stipulating that his widow and children and his son-in-law Chidiock Wardour should keep house together, provided his widow with the newly built great chamber on the back of the house and the furniture for it.[10] No doubt she could retreat there when the family became too much for her. It seems a sensible arrangement. Drew Saunders left his wife Anne four rooms, the little parlour, little buttery, little store, and little kitchen, in his house Moore-

---

[1] *Inq. p.m. Lond.*, i. 158–60.   [2] Ibid., ii. 105–9.
[3] Ibid., ii. 199–201.   [4] Ibid., iii. 36–7.
[5] Ibid., iii. 21.   [6] Ibid., iii. 58–60.
[7] P.C.C. 1 Carew, 31 Loftes, 34 Darcy, 57 Noodes.
[8] P.C.C. 31 Loftes.   [9] P.C.C. 57 Noodes.
[10] P.C.C. 10 Holney.

croftes in Hillingdon, Middlesex. His executors were to provide her and her maid with diet and if she wished to travel they were to provide her with two horses and a man, if she rode single, and with two horses and two men, if she rode double, but such travel was limited to 40 days in any one year.[1]

Such detailed provision was rare, for the more usual practice was to leave the widow part of the real property for life and part of the personal property absolutely. Thus Sir Andrew Judde left his wife Mary lands in Kent, Surrey, and Hertfordshire value £141 p.a. for life with reversion to his son John.[2] Similarly Sir George Barne left most of his London property, including two windmills in the suburbs, and his land in the country to his wife Alice for life.[3] Miles Mording did the same with his property in London and Staffordshire[4] and Sir John Gresham did the same with part of his large estates.[5] Justice demanded such dowers, for the husband had received his wife's portion at marriage.

The remainder of the real property and the reversion of the widow's share were usually divided among the merchant's sons. There were of course cases where one son alone, usually the eldest, inherited all the real property. Thus Edward Jackman seems to have left all his lands to his eldest son John, but subject to annuities of £20 to his younger sons Henry and Thomas and to annuities of an unspecified amount to his two daughters.[6] Francis Barnham left his land and houses in Surrey, Essex, and Wales to his third son Benedict, but he explained that his elder sons, Martin and Stephen, had already been 'sufficiently advanced' by him. Even so he left them £200 each.[7] Sole inheritance by the eldest son was only common where the property consisted of a single house. In other cases the property was usually divided among the sons, though not always equally. Thus Henry Herdson left one-third of his lands in Kent to his

[1] P.C.C. 26 Bakon.   [2] P.C.C. 54 Welles.

[3] P.C.C. 13 Noodes. One of the windmills was in Finsbury and the other on the Mount beyond St. Johns, cf. Stow, ii. 77, 80.

[4] P.C.C. 36 Chayre.   [5] P.C.C. 28 Ketchyn.

[6] P.C.C. 3 Lyon.   [7] P.C.C. 10 Carew.

eldest son and two-thirds to his four younger sons.[1] The division seems generally to have been more equal than that, but it is difficult to be certain about it. What is certain is that these London merchants, if they owned more than a single house, did not usually follow the rule of primogeniture in bequeathing their real property, whatever that disgruntled younger son, Thomas Wilson, may have said about that practice.[2]

Real property might constitute only a small part of a merchant's estate, for much of his wealth could consist of personal property. By the custom of London one-third of a citizen's personal property had to go to his widow, one-third to his children, and one-third to himself in the sense that he could dispose of that third as he wished. Where there were no children, the widow was entitled to half the personal property, and where there was no widow, the children were entitled to half. Wills show that this custom was generally maintained among the merchants, but it is difficult to tell from them the value of the different portions. The value of the two-thirds left to the widow and children is usually not specified. The value of the third portion might in theory be obtained by adding up all the separate bequests into which that portion was divided. That would be a laborious process and the total would not necessarily equal a third of the personal property, for the specific bequests are sometimes followed by the statement that the residue of that portion is left to the wife or the children. For the bigger estates however, where the bequests were given in detail, a rough calculation of the value of the third which the testator disposed of himself, gives some idea of the value of the other two-thirds which went to the widow and children, though in most cases such a calculation results in an under-estimate.

The widows of wealthy merchants were left very well off

[1] P.C.C. 38 More.

[2] T. Wilson, *The state of England*, ed. F. J. Fisher, Camden Society Miscellany, xvi. p. 24. Wilson was writing of the younger sons of esquires and gentlemen when he claimed that they did not share in the family inheritance, but was it even true in their case ?

under the terms of their husbands' wills. Thus Richard Chamberlain left 'my gentle Margaritt', his second wife, £2200. She was a widow with nine children when she married Chamberlain, so perhaps some of the money represented an earlier dower.[1] John Quarles left his second wife, Agnes, £2500 as her third part and an additional £500.[2] Edward Jackman's wife should have inherited at least £2600 as her third part and in addition she had a separate legacy of £200.[3] She was Anne, the daughter of Humphrey Packington, and her sister Jane, who married Humphrey Baskerfeld, should have inherited at least £2400 from him.[4] The third sister, Letitia, married Roger Martin, but she predeceased him, otherwise she might have inherited the £3000 or more which went to Martin's second wife, Elizabeth, daughter of William Castelin and widow of Thomas Knowles.[5] There were at least two other cases in which the share to which the widow was entitled exceeded £2000. Ralph Greneway, who died without issue, left half his personal estate to his wife Katherine and the other half in bequests to relatives, servants, and charity, which amounted to at least £2400.[6] A third of Henry Becher's personal property came to at least £2000, but his wife seems to have agreed not to take her third and to have received £1666 13s. 4d. instead.[7] Below the £2000 mark, the widows of William Bond and Anthony Gamage were entitled to at least £1400 and £1200 respectively.[8] Lower down the scale the numbers increase as the amounts decrease, but the evidence is too imperfect and incomplete to warrant any statistical analysis. It gives the impression that most merchants made provision for their wives during widowhood and that such provision was often substantial.

The allocation of equal parts of the personal estate to the widow and the children appears to put the latter at a disadvantage.

[1] P.C.C. 7 Stonarde ; S. Williams, *Letters written by John Chamberlain*, Camden Society, lxxix. p. ix.
[2] P.C.C. 3 Langley.　　　　　　　　[3] P.C.C. 3 Lyon.
[4] P.C.C. 9 Stevenson ; Overall, p. 21 n.
[5] P.C.C. 1 Martyn ; Overall, p. 308 n.　　　　　[6] P.C.C. F 30 Noodes.
[7] P.C.C. 10 Holney.　　　　　[8] P.C.C. 26 Carew, 32 Bakon.

The widow's third was undivided, the children's third might be shared among a number. Where the family was large and the estate small, the children's share of their third must have been very small indeed, though in practice young children were probably partly maintained out of the widow's dower in such cases. Moreover the children might have received a part of their father's personal property during his lifetime. Married daughters, who did not usually share the children's third, would have received their dowries and the older sons might already have been set up in business by their fathers. Finally children often received additional legacies from the third part which their father was free to dispose of as he wished.

The only son naturally came off best in this, but the only son was rare in that prolific age. Anthony Gamage's only son William was entitled to more than £1200 as his third[1] and Sir Lionel Duckett's only son Thomas to more than £600 despite his unfortunate marriage.[2] Where there was more than one child, the children seem usually to have shared equally in their third, though Francis Barnham left it entirely to his third son, to whom it was worth more than £800. That was unusual and it was expressly stated that Barnham had helped his two elder sons sufficiently during his lifetime.[3] The additional bequests to children, over and above their third, might vary, but Humphrey Baskerfeld left £200 to each of his sons and unmarried daughters, of whom there were seven including a child yet unborn.[4] Richard Mallory left his holding in the Russia Company equally among his six sons.[5] Edward Jackman, on the other hand, left £100 to each of his three sons and £200 to each of his two daughters.[6] Moreover sons had sometimes received substantial sums during their father's lifetime. Thus Sir Roger Martin's two sons, Humphrey and Edmund, had received £500 each ;[7] Sir Thomas Offley's son Hugh had received £200 on his marriage,[8] and two of Philip Gunter's

---

[1] P.C.C. 32 Bakon. [2] P.C.C. 9 Rutland. [3] P.C.C. 10 Carew.
[4] P.C.C. 9 Stevenson. [5] P.C.C. 9 Stonarde. [6] P.C.C. 3 Lyon.
[7] P.C.C. 1 Martyn. [8] P.C.C. 39 Tirwhite.

sons, Francis and Philip, had received £100 and £227 respectively.[1] Such sums were sometimes deducted from the recipient's share in the children's third. This seems to have been the case with the elder sons of John Quarles. Quarles made a rather complicated will, but it would seem that his eldest son John received £1050, his second son Benedict £800, his third son William £1050, and three younger children, Edward, Judith, and another John, received £1750 between them. These sums included money they had received during their father's lifetime.[2]

Not every member of the Russia Company could endow his sons as liberally as John Quarles did, but what is striking is not only the extent of the personal property members owned but also the way in which they distributed it among their children. That distribution was partly dictated by the custom of London, but even the disposal of the testator's own third showed little tendency towards primogeniture. Professor Tawney has suggested that ' the English family system . . . if it did not drown all the kittens but one, threw all but one into the water '.[3] If that is true of the younger sons of London merchants, they were at least endowed with fairly adequate lifebelts by their fathers. They had not to be content with ' that which the catt left on the malt heape ', to use Wilson's inelegant expression.[4]

The daughters were not forgotten either. Those who married during their fathers' lifetime received their dowries, which naturally varied with the wealth and standing of the father and the number of daughters he had to provide for. Thus Humphrey Baskerfeld's daughter had £200 on her marriage [5] and two of Richard Mallory's daughters had £200 and £266 13s. 4d. respectively.[6] William Bond, who seems to have had only one daughter, gave her a dowry of £1000 on her marriage to William Whitmore.[7] When Philip Gunter made his will in 1583

[1] P.C.C. 8 Rowe.   [2] P.C.C. 3 Langley.

[3] R. H. Tawney, ' The rise of the gentry, 1558–1640 ', *Economic History Review*, xi. 3.

[4] T. Wilson, *The state of England*, p. 24.   [5] P.C.C. 9 Stevenson.

[6] P.C.C. 9 Stonarde.   [7] P.C.C. 26 Carew.

he had four married daughters, three of whom had had dowries of £150 each and one had had a dowry of £200. Gunter stipulated that these sums should be deducted from the daughters' share of the children's third.[1] Married daughters do not seem often to have shared in that third, but they sometimes received separate legacies. Thus John Quarles left £450 to his daughter Anne Rickthorne, whose dowry had been £400, and £150 to his daughter Margaret Barker, whose dowry had been £200. He also left Margaret £16 p.a. Perhaps her husband had not been successful for he owed Quarles £290, a debt which was remitted.[2] Roger Martin also provided fairly amply for the three daughters of his second marriage. Two of them, Susan and Martha, had dowries of £336 13s. 4d. and legacies of £133 6s. 8d. each. The eldest, Mary, who had married Alexander Denton, had a dowry of £1000 and a legacy of £200, as well as £33 6s. 8d. for a ' billamente of golde '. Her husband received £80 for a gold chain.[3] Bequests to sons-in-law were not infrequent. Anthony Gamage left £50 to each of his four sons-in-law,[4] and John Spark left his ' freedome of Muscovy and newe trades ' to his son-in-law John Davenant.[5] Sons-in-law were sometimes given the custody of their wife's young brothers or sisters. Thus Harry Hungate, who married Humphrey Baskerfeld's daughter, was to bring up Baskerfeld's young child Sarah.[6]

The unmarried daughters had their share in the children's third, which was meant no doubt partly to provide them with maintenance and partly to provide them with dowries for their future marriages. Sir Rowland Heyward, for example, stipulated that his daughters' shares should be £1000 apiece.[7] The unmarried daughter also received specific bequests. Jackman's two unmarried daughters had £200 each,[8] William Lewkner's two had £40 each,[9] and Richard Mallory's four unmarried daughters had £60 each.[10] William Clifton left one unmarried

[1] P.C.C. 8 Rowe.	[2] P.C.C. 3 Langley.
[3] P.C.C. 1 Martyn.	[4] P.C.C. 32 Bakon.
[5] P.C.C. 3 Darcy.	[6] P.C.C. 9 Stevenson.
[7] P.C.C. 34 Darcy.	[8] P.C.C. 3 Lyon.
[9] P.C.C. 21 Welles.	[10] P.C.C. 9 Stonarde.

daughter £200 and another £100 and both were to share in ' the stock and gaines ' of his holding in the Russia Company, together with their two brothers and their married sister.[1] Indeed some provision for unmarried daughters seems to have been universal, though here again the custom of London demanded it.

Bequests of personal property to other relatives naturally depended in part on the size of the estate and the existence of a widow, sons, and daughters who had a claim on that estate. It seems to have been rare to make bequests to parents, perhaps because, when a man came to make his will in the sixteenth century, his parents were usually dead. There were however some pleasing examples of such bequests. William Dawkes, who had two daughters but no son, left £45 to his father and mother, who lived at Droitwich, a black gown to his mother, his best gelding with the best saddle and bridle, his best gown, coat and doublet to his father, and to both of them jointly a butt of good malmsey every year for the rest of their lives.[2] Henry Fallowfield left £5 to his mother-in-law.[3] Brothers and sisters, nephews and nieces, and the indefinable cousins tended to gain most when the testator had no issue of his own. Thus Ralph Greneway, who died without issue, left £500 to his brother Thomas of Cley in Norfolk, £300 to one sister and £50 to another, and £1150 to various nephews and nieces.[4] Robert Wolman, who also had no children, left £10 p.a. to one cousin and his freedom, claim, and interest in the Russia Company to another.[5] Even when the testator had children, he sometimes left useful legacies to other relatives. Edward Jackman, after providing for his children, left £100 to his brother Thomas, £20 to each of two unmarried sisters, and £700 to nephews and nieces. The brother and one sister lived in Buckinghamshire and the other sister in Gloucestershire.[6] Such bequests were not made only by men of large estate, for the less wealthy made them too, and they sometimes suggest the country background of the London merchant family.

[1] P.C.C. 34 Stevenson.
[2] P.C.C. 31 More.
[3] P.C.C. 17 Crymes.
[4] P.C.C. F. 30 Noodes.
[5] P.C.C. 8 Holney.
[6] P.C.C. 3 Lyon.

Bequests to brothers and sisters and nephews and nieces had to be made from the testator's own third of his personal estate. The original idea behind the triple division was that the citizen, having provided for his widow and his children, should have a third of his personal property to spend for the good of his soul. Though the religious significance of the division had declined by the second half of the sixteenth century, the disposal of the testator's own third of his personal property has a special interest. The bequests made out of that third not only give some indication of the total value of the personal estate, but they show the sort of things a merchant was interested in and wished to support. It would be claiming too much to say that they provide a glimpse into the mind of the merchant, but they show something of the mental climate of his age and perhaps also of his class. The bequests to relatives suggest a strong feeling for the family and for the ties of kinship. The bequests to servants suggest a patriarchal attitude more often associated with the country than with the urban household. Relatives and servants might have a special claim to consideration, the former by blood and the latter by service, but bequests to those who had not such claims show clearly the merchant's attitude to some of the institutions of his day.

The third of his estate, which the merchant disposed of for the good of his soul, might have been expected to provide substantial bequests to the church, which had the cure of that soul, but one of the most striking features of merchants' wills is the infrequency and smallness of such bequests. Even the wealthy merchants left little to the church. Richard Chamberlain stipulated that he should be buried in the church of St. Olave, where his first wife was buried, but he left only £10 to that church.[1] Edward Jackman left £10 to the church of St. Peter the Poor and £5 to the church at Hornchurch, Essex.[2] Sir Thomas Offley elaborately stipulated that, if he died in London, he should be buried in St. Andrew Undershaft in the middle of the chancel on the north side of the middle aisle, near the place where his first wife

[1] P.C.C. 7 Stonarde.   [2] P.C.C. 3 Lyon.

Joan was buried. He left 5s. 8d. to the parson of St. Andrew for tithes negligently forgotten.[1] Sir George Barne was one of the few members of the company who left real property to the church. He bequested two small tenements to the churchwardens of St. Bartholomew the Little, the income from which was to be used to provide holy bread and to provide for the poor.[2]

Such bequests to the church, whether of real or of personal property, were exceptional, but one form of bequest was more common. Merchants often left money for a funeral sermon or a series of sermons. Henry Becher left £6 for ten sermons [3] and Edward Jackman £20 for four preachers to deliver ten sermons each.[4] These should have been good sermons for the preachers were paid above the standard rate, which was clearly 6s. 8d. a sermon.[5] Thus Sir Roger Martin left £6 13s. 4d. for twenty sermons to be preached in the Mercers Chapel [6] and Sir John Rivers left the same amount to the churchwardens of Hadlow, Kent, for four sermons p.a. for five years.[7] Finally Philip Gunter left £13 6s. 8d. to the churchwardens of St. Michael, Cornhill, for two sermons p.a. at 6s. 8d. each ' for evermore so longe as the worlde shall endure '.[8] On the whole it was the richer merchants who provided for sermons in which no doubt their virtues were extolled. The Elizabethans certainly do not seem to have shared their Queen's views about sermons.

Though legacies to the church were few and small, it might be said that the endowment of education was an indirect way of assisting a church whose links with the universities and the schools were very close. Certainly the members of the Russia Company showed more interest in education than they did in the church itself. Apart from the more spectacular benefactions,

---

[1] P.C.C. 39 Tirwhite.
[2] P.C.C. 13 Noodes. Some members who made their wills during Mary's reign left lands to the church, e.g. Sir Robert Rochester (P.C.C. F. 15 Welles) and Sir John Gage (P.C.C. 9 Ketchyn). Such cases were rare.
[3] P.C.C. 10 Holney.   [4] P.C.C. 3 Lyon.
[5] John Kempe, brother of the charter member of that name, left money for 300 sermons at 6s. 8d. each (P.C.C. 23 Sheffeld).
[6] P.C.C. 1 Martyn.   [7] P.C.C. 37 Butts.   [8] P.C.C. 8 Rowe.

as Sir Thomas White's foundation of St. John's College, Oxford, and Sir Thomas Gresham's foundation of the college in London which bears his name, there was a fairly steady stream of legacies to the two universities. Such legacies came almost wholly from the richer merchants and they were usually in sums of from £20 to £40, equally divided between Oxford and Cambridge. Some were left specifically for the assistance of poor scholars in divinity. Very few indeed of these bequests came from men who had themselves been at either university.

A limited number of schools also benefited from the wealth of members of the company. Sir Thomas White helped to found the Merchant Taylors School and Sir Andrew Judde founded the grammar school at Tonbridge, for which he left property to provide the master with a salary of £20 p.a. and the usher one of £8 p.a.[1] Robert Wolman left property in London and Middlesex for the erection and endowment of a school at Uxbridge,[2] and William Dawkes left £40 for building and £10 p.a. for endowing a free school at Droitwich.[3] Sir Rowland Heyward left £20 p.a. to his old school at Bridgnorth.[4] The school which appealed most to London merchants was clearly Christ's Hospital, which received a number of bequests, mostly from the wealthier members. At least two dozen members left money to Christ's Hospital, in sums ranging from £100 to £2. Thus education gained more than the church from the wealth of merchants, but it was not lavishly endowed considering the extent of that wealth.

The merchant's link with the universities and the schools may have been slight, especially if his own education had been largely through apprenticeship begun at an early age, but his link with London and its companies was close and direct. Few members of the Russia Company, however, left money for improving the city's amenities. William Bond left £500 to the city for buying

---

[1] P.C.C. 54 Welles ; Stow, i. 113.   [2] P.C.C. 8 Holney.

[3] P.C.C. F 31 More ; *V.C.H. Worcestershire*, iv. 529.

[4] W. Jay, ' Sir Rowland Hayward ', *Trans. London and Middlesex Archaeological Society*, N.S. vi. 522.

wheat, but this was only to be paid if his children's shares turned out to be £2000 each.[1] Two members showed an interest in the city's water supply. Edward Jackman and David Woodroff were 'benefactors towardes the water conduites' for which they left £100 and £20 respectively.[2] Perhaps Sir Christopher Draper should be included among such benefactors, for he left £20 for repairing and cleansing the Thames. Draper also left £60 for improving the roads between London and Langley in Hertfordshire.[3] Such roads apparently needed attention for Sir John Gresham declared that the roads within 20 miles of London were 'most noysome and fowle', and he left £50 for repairing them.[4] Such bequests did not amount to very much, and indeed merchants who wished to improve roads and bridges preferred to do so in their native counties or in the country places where they had settled. Thus Francis Barnham left £5 for repairing the roads near Southwick in Hampshire,[5] Philip Gunter £30 for the roads from Monmouth to Brecknock,[6] and Humphrey Baskerfeld £6 13s. 4d. for repairing three bridges in Worcestershire.[7] In the last two cases, and probably in the first also, it was the native county that was to benefit. Others may have hoped to benefit their heirs as well as the public in general by this sort of bequest. William Clifton, for example, left £20 for mending the highways within 20 miles of his house at Barrington, Somerset.[8] Whatever the motive for such bequests, the mending of roads cannot have provided a very permanent memorial of the benefactor.

London did not figure prominently as a recipient of legacies from members of the company perhaps because it was too large and anonymous to inspire gratitude in men whose loyalty was more strongly aroused by smaller and more intimate groupings.

---

[1] P.C.C. 26 Carew. [2] P.C.C. 3 Lyon, 21 Chayre ; Stow, i. 18–19.
[3] P.C.C. 22 Darcy. [4] P.C.C. 28 Ketchyn.
[5] P.C.C. 10 Carew. [6] P.C.C. 8 Rowe.
[7] P.C.C. 9 Stevenson. John Quarles left £50 for repairing a Norfolk bridge (P.C.C. 3 Langley).
[8] P.C.C. 34 Stevenson. Sir William Cordell left £6 13s. 4d. for repairing the roads at Long Melford, Suffolk, where he lived, and £10 for repairing Borley bridge (P.C.C. 42 Darcy).

Certainly the contrast between the bequests to the city and the bequests to the city companies is very marked. Almost every merchant of any wealth and standing, who was a member of the Russia Company and of a livery company, left something to his livery company. Such bequests were of three types. Firstly members left pieces of plate to their companies, the bowls, the standing cups, and the silver spoons with the donor's monogram on the handles. Such plate formed a permanent memorial, but some benefactors were not satisfied with that. Philip Gunter ordered his executors within a year of his death to get a ' scutchion ' made with his arms on it and have it set up in the Skinners' Hall ' like as Sir Andrew Judde's was set up '.[1] Secondly, members left money to their companies without specifying how it should be used, as Richard Chamberlain left £50 to the Ironmongers.[2] Such bequests, though fairly common, do not often seem to have been as large as Chamberlain's. Finally members left money to their companies and stipulated how that money should be used.

Members who left money to their livery companies for a particular purpose usually stipulated that it should be used in one of two ways. The most frequent bequests were of sums of money to provide a dinner for the company, as when Sir George Barne left £20 to the Haberdashers for a dinner on the day of his burial.[3] The sums varied from £2 to £40. Sir Roger Martin left £40 to the Mercers for a dinner on the day of his burial for the whole company with as many of their wives as they could conveniently place. Martin seems to have been a strong believer in this form of commemoration for he also left £6 13s. 4d. to the ' poor waterbearers company ' for a dinner for themselves and their wives, and £10 for a dinner for his ' loving neighbours '.[4]

---

[1] P.C.C. 8 Rowe.   Gunter's executors were also to provide him with a marble tomb with two ' scutchions ' bearing the arms of himself and his wife ' graven in copper '.

[2] P.C.C. 7 Stonarde.   [3] P.C.C. 13 Noodes.

[4] P.C.C. 1 Martyn.   Francis Barnham left £2 to the clothiers of Guildford and Basingstoke respectively ' to make them a dinner ', which probably indicates his business connexions (P.C.C. 10 Carew).

It seems probable that the dinners were usually confined to the livery of the company, for Henry Becher, after making the usual bequest to the Haberdashers for a dinner, left a separate 5 marks to the yeomanry for that purpose.[1] All this was a convivial but hardly a lasting way of commemorating the deceased.

These legacies devoted to consumption goods were less important than the other type of earmarked bequest in which the money was to be used by the company to provide loans to its young members. In these cases the sums were larger and the benefit more lasting. These bequests ranged from £100 to £400 and the money was to be loaned to young men in sums ranging from £13 6s. 8d. to £50. The testator always specified the size of the individual loans and how long they could be held, which was anything from two to seven years. He sometimes stipulated that the first loans should be made to his relatives or apprentices or servants. Thus Humphrey Baskerfeld in leaving £200 to the Mercers for loans laid it down that the first loans should go to his kindred if they were free of the Mercers Company. If they were not so free, then his apprentice, Richard Cupper, was to have a loan of £50.[2] Anthony Gamage, who left £400 to the Ironmongers for loans, stipulated that his brothers-in-law, John and Richard Woodward, should have the first use of £300, and his apprentices, Peter Johnson and James Lorde, the first use of the remaining £100.[3] Afterwards the money was to be shared among ten young men who were to pay 1½ per cent interest. Others, as Philip Gunter[4] and Edward Jackman,[5] stipulated that no interest should be taken. Others again specified the rate of interest and how that interest should be used. The £200 which Roger Martin bequeathed to the Mercers was to be lent at 4 per cent and the interest given to four London prisons.[6] Humphrey Baskerfeld, who also left £200 to the Mercers but in a will that was made before the Act of 1571 had legalized the taking of interest, stipulated that the four young men who

---

[1] P.C.C. 10 Holney. [2] P.C.C. 9 Stevenson.
[3] P.C.C. 32 Bakon. [4] P.C.C. 8 Rowe.
[5] P.C.C. 3 Lyon. [6] P.C.C. 1 Martyn.

borrowed the £200 should each in return deliver two loads of charcoal p.a., which was to be distributed among the poor.[1]

These loans were obviously intended for young men setting up in business on their own. Philip Gunter, in leaving £100 to the Skinners for loans, laid it down that priority should be given to borrowers who were young beginners in upholstery,[2] and Roger Martin stipulated that his £200 should be lent to young mercers who were not in the livery.[3] Provision for such loans was common, though it was rarely done on the grand scale of Sir Thomas White's endowment of loans to be enjoyed by twenty-three provincial towns in turn. Such provision shows both the need for capital and a cheap and convenient source from which that need could be satisfied.

The money left to livery companies for loans might be an indirect way of helping the poor, when the interest from such loans was devoted to charity. Such provision was, however, rare, for most loans seem to have been interest free, and the merchant who wished to leave money for the poor usually did so directly. The bequests made to the poor by members of the Russia Company were many and varied. The institutions which commonly received legacies were the London hospitals of St. Thomas and St. Bartholomew and the London prisons, which received money for the poor prisoners. Edward Jackman left £40 to Bridewell and £5 to Bedlam,[4] and Ralph Greneway £8 to six lazar houses near London,[5] but such bequests were rare. Both Francis Barnham and John Quarles left money for the poor of the French and Dutch churches and the latter left £5 for the poor people of the congregation of Italians.[6] Many bequests were made to the poor of the parish in which the testator lived or of the ward which he represented as alderman. Thus David Woodroff left £10 to the poor of St. Andrew's parish where

---

[1] P.C.C. 9 Stevenson. The wording of the will is rather obscure, but it seems to mean that the four borrowers should pay two loads of charcoal each, not two loads in all.

[2] P.C.C. 8 Rowe.   [3] P.C.C. 1 Martyn.
[4] P.C.C. 3 Lyon.   [5] P.C.C. F 30 Noodes.   [6] P.C.C. 3 Langley.

he dwelt,[1] and Sir Thomas Offley left £10 to the poor house-holders of Aldgate Ward of which he was an alderman.[2]
There was a tendency, too, to spread bequests over a large number of poor as if to make the circle of gratitude as wide as possible. This was not wholly disinterested, for the giving of black gowns to large numbers of the poor was meant to contribute to the pomp and circumstance of the benefactor's funeral. Thus Philip Gunter left gowns to 92 poor men who were to attend his funeral in them,[3] and Sir Roger Martin left 100 marks for 100 gowns for 100 men and women who were to do the same.[4] Sir Thomas Lodge left 2s. and a new pair of gloves for each of 78 poor men who were to attend his funeral.[5] It was important to leave this world with ceremony however unobtrusive the entry into it might have been. Similarly another favourite bequest, that of money for 'poor maids' marriages', was spread over a large number of grateful recipients. Thus both Ralph Greneway [6] and John Quarles [7] left £33 6s. 8d. for 100 poor maids' marriages, which was 6s. 8d. apiece, or the price of a sermon. That seems to have been the standard rate, though occasionally poor maidens got as much as 10s.
Bequests also show a certain geographical dispersion, as when Quarles left money to the poor of nine places in four counties.[8] Such dispersion might show the places where the testator owned property or did business, but it usually indicated where he had come from or where he had settled after making his money in London. Thus Humphrey Baskerfeld left £6 to the poor of Wolverley where he was born,[9] and Philip Gunter left money for poor maids' marriages and for coal for 25 poor men in his native Monmouthshire.[10] Sir Roger Martin bequeathed £66 13s. 4d. for 200 poor householders in Long Melford where he was born and £10 to the poor of Hoxton where he

---

[1] P.C.C. 21 Chayre.   [2] P.C.C. 39 Tirwhite.
[3] P.C.C. 8 Rowe.   [4] P.C.C. 1 Martyn.
[5] P.C.C. 39 Brudenell.   [6] P.C.C. F 30 Noodes.
[7] P.C.C. 3 Langley.   [8] Ibid.
[9] P.C.C. 9 Stevenson.   [10] P.C.C. 8 Rowe.

maintained a house.[1] It was a pleasant feature of the local boy who had made good that he should thus remember his native place. These charitable bequests, made for the good of the soul, were no doubt meant to smooth the path to heaven. As Richard Chamberlain's epitaph put it :

> To the pore he was liberall and gave for God's sake,
> But now his fame is plentifull and he a hevenly make.[2]

Men might give ' for God's sake ', but their bequests were usually for secular purposes. Even so it would be cynical to regard such bequests merely as conscience money, for men had a genuine compassion for the poor and did not consider that the establishment of a state system of poor relief, based on statute and a compulsory poor rate, absolved them from the duty of private charity. Still less did worldly success absolve a man from his responsibilities to his family. In a sense it increased those responsibilities, for the children must make marriages and the sons must engage in business appropriate to the position achieved by the father. No doubt such matters seemed more important to the wealthy than to the poorer merchants, but the hierarchical society meant in practice one in which men did not think that they must not or could not rise in the social scale, but one in which they felt that they must not fall.

[1] P.C.C. 1 Martyn.   [2] Stow, ii. 335.

CHAPTER V

CONCLUSION

A STUDY of the members of the Russia Company shows that they consisted of men—and two women—drawn from different ranks of society. The presence in a trading company of so many nobles and holders of high office was exceptional and arose probably from the exploratory nature of the initial enterprise and from the joint-stock form of its capital. These men do not seem to have played a large part in the company's affairs or to have been themselves actively interested in the conduct of foreign trade. The majority of members, however, appear to have been London merchants who were actively engaged in foreign trade. Such merchants had certain common interests and activities, which were probably common also to the merchant class as a whole. Some of them became rich and left their families fairly richly endowed. Such riches suggest the interesting and difficult question whether there was continuity in these merchant families in the sense of the sons carrying on their fathers' businesses or indeed in the sense of the father himself continuing in trade once he had achieved a certain degree of opulence.

The question was clearly not one of wealth alone, for there might be no sons to continue in trade in that age of heavy mortality. Most members of the Russia Company who can be identified had sons living at the time of their deaths, though such sons were sometimes young and may not have reached manhood. The evidence gives the impression, though it is nothing more than an impression, that failure of the direct line was less common than it had been among the merchant class of medieval London.[1] Moreover where sons inherited chiefly personal property or real property in the form of shops, cellars, and warehouses, that might form an added inducement to remain in trade.

[1] S. L. Thrupp, *The merchant class of medieval London*, pp. 198–206.

What form the personal property took, especially in the larger estates, it is difficult to say. Household goods and plate accounted for a little. There might be a stock of goods in England, like the cloth which Sir Thomas White owned, and abroad, like the goods in Spain which Sir George Barne's servant was to gather up. There was capital in the Russia Company and sometimes in the Mineral and Battery Works and the Mines Royal, and sometimes, most unhappily, in Frobisher's north-west ventures. There was money out on loan, sometimes to the Queen at 10 per cent, sometimes to private individuals, who, if they were relatives of the lender, might be lucky enough to have their debts forgiven at his death. Some of this personal estate, the ships, the goods, perhaps even the goodwill, might yield the best return if the legatee continued to employ it himself in trade.

The merchant making his will often provided for the continuance of his business by his widow or his children. Thus in 1576 William Bond left Crosby Place to his wife Margaret for life, who was to live there and jointly continue in the trade of merchandise. Presumably she was to trade jointly with her second son, William, then aged about 19, for if she married again the house was to go to William, not to the eldest son Daniel, who seems to have been a parson.[1] Three years later Margaret Bond, widow, and William Bond were charter members of the Eastland Company.[2] Similarly Robert Dawbeney left his house, shop, and cellars to Elizabeth, his wife, for life with reversion to his eldest son Arthur. He also left £3 and a gown to Edmund Brudnell desiring and praying him to help his, Dawbeney's, wife in her business.[3] Arthur traded with Barbary and later became a member of the Spanish and Barbary Companies.[4] He seems to have been of age when his father died, but it was not unknown for widows to continue in trade even when they had grown-up sons.

[1] P.C.C. 26 Carew ; *Inq. p.m. Lond.*, iii. 133–5. Daniel, who was not knighted, is referred to as Sir Daniel in his father's will.

[2] S.P.D. Eliz., cxxxi. no. 70.   [3] P.C.C. 57 Noodes.

[4] Exch. K.R. Port Books, 2/1, 6/3 ; Patent Rolls, 19 Eliz., pt. 8 ; Hakluyt, iv. 268.

Naturally there was continuity in many merchant families such as the Barnes, the Bonds, the Castelins, and the Garroways. Such continuity is shown in the membership of the Russia Company itself. Sir George Barne's eldest son, George, was several times a governor of the company [1] and Richard Barne, one of the company's agents in the early seventeenth century, seems to have been George's son.[2] William Merick's son, John, was one of the most prominent members of the company in the early seventeenth century, when he was an agent in Russia, an ambassador to Russia, and finally a governor of the company.[3] Walter Garroway's brother William was a member of the company at the end of the sixteenth century,[4] and William's son, Sir Henry, was a governor in 1643.[5] Finally Richard Foulkes's eldest son, Austin, was an agent in Russia in the fifteen-eighties, though it is not certain that he was also a member of the company.[6]

Such continuity seems most common where the families were either not very rich or where, being fairly rich, their wealth was chiefly in the form of personal property. Those who inherited or bought land were sometimes tempted to leave the city and become country gentlemen. Thus William Clifton of London, gentleman and merchant tailor in 1547,[7] bought the manor of Barrington in Somerset three years later [8] and by 1559 was described as 'late of London'.[9] When he made his will in 1562 he was William Clifton of Barrington, but he still held his stock in the Russia Company and was also a partner with Lionel Duckett in a licence and stock of £750 for the buying and merchandising of felts.[10] Edmund Lomnour, who seems to have

[1] S.P.D. Eliz., ccxxxviii, no. 129 ; *C.S.P.D. 1591-4*, p. 170 ; *C.S.P. For. 1584-5*, pp. 132, 222 ; Hakluyt, ii. 203.

[2] *H.M.C. Salisbury*, xi. 386, xii. 421-2, 425 ; Hasted, p. 160.

[3] *D.N.B.*, Overall, p. 13.

[4] S.P. Foreign Russia, i. ff. 118, 194.   [5] Johnson, iii. 143.

[6] P.C.C. 38 Lyon ; G. Tolstoy, *The first forty years of intercourse between England and Russia, 1553-1593* (St. Petersburg, 1875), pp. 290, 295, 362.

[7] *C.P.R. 1547-8*, p. 148.   [8] Ibid. *1550-3*, p. 416.

[9] Ibid. *1558-60*, p. 236.   [10] P.C.C. 34 Stevenson.

been a customs official rather than a merchant, died as a country gentleman at Mannington, Norfolk, leaving much property and some cattle to his wife.[1]   Similarly Henry Brunker died as a well-to-do country gentleman of Erlestock in Wiltshire,[2] but his interest in trade may have been limited to his membership of the Russia Company.

The anonymous author of 'An apologie of the cittie of London' pointed out that Londoners were ' by birth for the most part of a mixture of all countries' of the realm, and that the merchants and rich men among them ' being satisfyed with gaine, doe for the most part marry theyr children into the countrey, and convey themselves after Ciceroes counsell, *veluti ex portu in agros et possessiones*'.[3]   That may be true, but a study of the members of the Russia Company suggests that, though some of them came from the provinces, few of them retired altogether from London.   Some, as David Woodroff, Sir John Branche, and Sir Roger Martin, maintained a house in London and a house in the provinces.   That might be a half-way stage to complete withdrawal, but it would be rash to conclude that it was so. Richard Mallory, who seems to have maintained his town and country house, was careful to stipulate that his eldest son should be apprenticed to ' an honest merchant ' and his second son to ' an honest man '.[4]   It is true that the children sometimes married ' into the countrey '.   Thus Sir Rowland Heyward married as his second wife ' Customer Smithe his daughter, a grave matron of xvi yeres '.[5]   She bore him eight children in twelve years of whom six survived infancy.   Of the six, four were daughters all of whom married country gentlemen ; of the two sons, the younger, John, settled in Kent and the elder, George, probably remained in London.   He died childless at the age of 28.[6]

---

[1] P.C.C. F 50 Noodes.   [2] P.C.C. 15 Babington.
[3] Stow, ii. 207–8.   [4] P.C.C. 9 Stonarde.
[5] E. Lodge, *Illustrations of British history*, ii. 244.   The grave matron was Catherine, daughter of Thomas Smith and his wife Alice, daughter of Sir Andrew Judde.
[6] W. Jay, ' Sir Rowland Hayward ', *Trans. London and Middlesex Archaeological Society*, N.S. vi. 522.

No one would deny that merchants changed 'estate with gentlemen' as Harrison put it and that some of them founded county families, but the number, and especially the proportion, of such transformations may well be exaggerated. Most members of the Russia Company who were merchants seem to have remained merchants in London and their sons also. They probably had neither the wish nor the resources to do anything else. Certainly some who had the resources did not apparently wish to turn themselves into country gentry. The very few who not only bought landed estates, which after all might only be a form of investment, but also abandoned trade and London itself, appear to be quite exceptional. The trouble with exceptions is just that they are exceptional and therefore tend to be better known than the general run of mankind.

It might be argued that any analysis of the members of a trading company was really an analysis of the exceptional members, those whose wealth and ability were above the average. There is some truth in such an argument and in the view that economic history tends to become 'the retrospective consecration of success'. It is easy to see why this should be so. The successful leave traces of their success, the failures are often buried with their failure. Not only do contemporaries sometimes record and applaud the materially successful, so that even John Stow sometimes reads like an Elizabethan Samuel Smiles, but the materially successful leave behind them monuments, not only in stone and marble, but in paper and parchment. Such monuments form the material of history by which the historian is bound, unless he wishes to qualify for the chief garblership, not of spices, but of sources.

It must be admitted that a study of the charter members of the Russia Company is exposed to these dangers and limitations. It tends to emphasize the more wealthy and successful members, though it should be remembered that such men played a greater part in the trade and life of London than did their less successful fellows. It raises problems of identification which cannot always be solved. It poses questions of family history which cannot always be answered. Despite these difficulties, such a study can give some picture of a group of London merchants who were not without importance in their time. It may even make some contribution to that large and neglected subject, the merchant class of Tudor London, which still awaits its historian.

BIOGRAPHICAL APPENDIX [1]

Thomas Allen. It is impossible to be certain of Allen's identity. He was probably the Thomas Allen, a member of the Skinners Company,[2] who was granted ' the office of queen's merchant in the East parts beyond the seas ' on 20 June 1561.[3] In 1565 he was exporting cloth to Danzig [4] and in 1567 importing cables and linen from Amsterdam and hemp, linen, fish, and poldavies from Danzig.[5] He operated a rope walk at Woolwicn [6] and owned a ship engaged in the wool trade with Bruges.[7] He seems to have been an assistant in the Russia Company in 1569.[8] He died at the end of 1591 or the beginning of 1592 leaving property in London and Kent and goods and debts due to him beyond the seas.[9]

William Allen. He was probably the William Allen who was alderman, 1559–86, mayor in 1571–2, knighted in 1571, and who died in 1586. Originally a member of the Leathersellers Company, of which he was master in 1558–9, he later transferred to the Mercers Company of which he was four times master.[10] He was a charter assistant in the Russia Company and apparently a member in 1570.[11] His trading interests were wide for he was a merchant adventurer [12] shipping cloth to Danzig, Emden, Antwerp, and Vigo in 1565 [13] and importing prunes from Nantes and wine from Spain in 1567–8.[14] He was a charter member of the Spanish Company of 1577.[15]

John Amcotes. A John Amcotes was importing wine in 1553–4.[16] He

---

[1] This appendix gives the names of all the charter members of the Russia Company. Some of the members are included in the *D.N.B.*, and in their cases the biographies that follow consist only of information which supplements or corrects the accounts in the *D.N.B.*

[2] Lambert, pp. 67, 194, 251.

[3] *C.P.R. 1560–3*, p. 127 ; cf. R. Ascham, *Works*, ed. J. A. Giles, ii. 39.

[4] Exch. K.R. Port Books, 2/1.　　　　　　　　　　[5] Smit, ii. 980–1.

[6] Hasted, p. 155 n.　　　[7] *A.P.C. 1581–2*, pp. 83–4.　　　[8] Hakluyt, ii. 86.

[9] P.C.C. 27 Harrington ; *C.S.P.D. 1591–4*, p. 175.

[10] Beaven, ii. 36.　　　　　[11] *C.S.P. Colonial, East Indies, 1513–1616*, p. 8.

[12] *C.S.P.D. 1547–80*, p. 267.

[13] Exch. K.R. Port Books, 2/1 ; cf. Smit, ii. 1077.

[14] Exch. K.R. Port Books, 4/2.

[15] Patent Rolls, 19 Eliz., pt. 8.

[16] Exch. K.R. Customs Accounts, 86/2.

was probably a member of the Amcotes family of Astrop, Lincs, and may have been the John Amcotes of Astrop who died in 1557.[1]

Thomas Anderson. He may have been the Thomas Anderson, citizen and fishmonger, who leased watermills 'called Crasshe Mylles in Estsmythfeld by the Tower of London' [2] in 1562. In 1598 a Henry Anderson was a member of the Russia Company.[3]

Edmund Ansell. In 1541 he was 'servaunt and factor' of Henry Herdson, skinner, in Spain.[4] He was himself a skinner and by 1553–4, when he was importing canvas,[5] he seems to have been trading on his own account. In the 'sixties and 'seventies he was exporting cloth to Vigo, bays to San Lucar, and Welsh cotton to Rouen, from which he imported Normandy glass.[6] He was a charter member of the Spanish Company of 1577,[7] and died in August 1585, leaving unspecified personal property to his wife Christian, who was to give some reasonable portion to the church and poor of St. Mary Woolchurch.[8]

Davie Appowell. He was a mercer [9] engaged in exporting cloth in 1547 and 1553–4 and importing friezadoes in 1553–4 and 1556–7.[10] He left £100 to the Mercers Company for loans, the interest on which was to be paid in coals for the poor of St. Lawrence parish.[11]

Henry, earl of Arundel, lord steward of the household.[12]

Thomas Atkinson, notary public. He was probably 'master Atkynson the skrevener', whose three daughters were married on 14 July 1560.[13] In 1569 he was an assistant of the Russia Company.[14] He died about

---

[1] P.C.C. 25 Wrastley. He was probably related to Henry Amcotes, alderman, 1536–54, mayor, 1548–9 (Beaven, ii. 30), who was a son of William Amcotes of Astrop (Machyn, p. 339).　　　　[2] *C.P.R. 1560–3*, p. 245.

[3] S.P. Foreign Russia, i. f. 118.　　　　[4] Marsden, i. 112–13.

[5] Exch. K.R. Customs Accounts, 86/2.

[6] Exch. K.R. Port Books, 2/1, 4/2, 6/4.

[7] Patent Rolls, 19 Eliz., pt. 8.　　　　[8] P.C.C. 40 Brudenell.

[9] *C.P.R. 1557–8*, p. 348, which records a debt of 100 marks due to him.

[10] Exch. K.R. Customs Accounts, 86/2, 6, 87/4, 167/1.

[11] W. Herbert, *History of the twelve great livery companies of London*, i. 287.

[12] *D.N.B.*, Henry Fitzalan, 12th earl of Arundel, 1511?–1580.

[13] Machyn, p. 240. They were probably the children of his first wife, Parnel (P.C.C. 4 Peter).

[14] Hakluyt, ii. 86.

two years later, leaving his personal estate to his second wife, Anne, to his eight children under age, and to a child unborn.[1]

Nicholas Bacon.[2] Bacon's family connexions, his official career culminating in the lord keepership, and his acquisition of monastic property are well known. He was a cloth exporter in the 'forties and 'fifties.[3] His memorandum of 5 April 1564 on the trade with Narva shows a good knowledge of and a sound approach to commercial problems.[4]

Thomas Bannister. Bannister was a member of the Skinners Company of which he was master warden in 1563[5] and he may have been M.P. for Reigate in 1558.[6] In the 'fifties he was a merchant adventurer[7] exporting cloth to Danzig and Denmark and importing raisins and Bilbao iron, presumably from Spain.[8] He also imported felts from Spain and figs from Portugal in both of which countries he seems to have kept a servant or factor.[9] He was one of the promoters of the third Guinea voyage of 1558 and part owner of the *Christopher Bennett* employed on that voyage.[10] About ten years later he was insuring goods in the Anglo-French trade.[11] Bannister seems to have been a fairly important member of the Russia Company. He was concerned in the commission of 17 May 1553 for pressing men for the first voyage[12] and was an assistant in 1569.[13] In 1568 he went out to Russia with the ambassador, Thomas Randolph, to investigate the company's affairs, to give advice on the renewal of its privileges, and to act as an agent for the fifth voyage to Persia. After restoring order among the company's servants and helping to get new privileges, Bannister went on to Persia where he died on 29 July 1571.[14] He left a 'mansion house' in London, which was to be sold and the money divided among his three sons and three daughters.[15]

---

[1] P.C.C. 4 Peter, where he is described as citizen and writer of the court letter of the city of London.   [2] *D.N.B.*, Sir Nicholas Bacon, 1509–1579.
[3] Exch. K.R. Customs Accounts, 86/2, 87/4, 167/1 ; S.P.D. Eliz., vi. no. 52.
[4] S.P.D. Eliz., xxxiii. no. 42.   [5] Lambert, pp. 67, 216.
[6] C. G. Bayne, ' The first house of commons of Queen Elizabeth ', *E.H.R.*, xxiii. 671.   [7] Smit, i. 757.
[8] Exch. K.R. Customs Accounts, 86/2, 6, 87/4 ; *A.P.C. 1550–2*, p. 365 ; *C.S.P. For. 1553–8*, p. 168.
[9] *C.S.P. For. 1561–2*, pp. 176, 307–8 ; H.C.A. Examinations, 11 (27 Jan. 1557).
[10] Blake, ii. 430–1 ; H.C.A. Libels, 37. no. 247, Examinations, 13 (20 Jan. 1560).
[11] H.C.A. Examinations, 16 (14 Jan. 1568).
[12] H.C.A. Exemplifications, 5. f. 157.   [13] Hakluyt, ii. 86.
[14] Add. MSS. 35831, f. 276 ; Hakluyt, ii. 119–25 ; Morgan and Coote, ii. 258–64, 283–4.
[15] P.C.C. 1 Carew. He left a gold ring to his cousin, Thomas Nicholes, clerk to the Merchant Adventurers.

Sir George Barne,[1] **knight and alderman.** He was the son of George Barne, grocer of London, and married Alice Brooke of Shropshire. Of his children, his son George married Anne, daughter of Sir William Garrard, Elizabeth married Sir John Rivers, and Anne married firstly Alexander Carleill and secondly Sir Francis Walsingham.[2] The Pardon Roll of 1547 describes Barne comprehensively as ' alderman, innholder or vintner of London, alias late of Wells, Somerset, blacksmith, alias late sheriff of London, alias citizen and haberdasher of London '.[3] He was in fact a member of the Haberdashers Company, an alderman, 1542–58, mayor in 1552–3, and knighted on 11 April 1553 ; he died 18 February 1558 [4]

Barne was one of the chief promoters of the Russia voyage of 1553 [5] and was a charter consul of the company, in whose affairs he played an active part. He was one of the signatories to a commission of 10 December 1556 for the recovery of goods from the *Edward Bonaventure*, wrecked on the Scottish coast on its return from Russia.[6] With four other members he signed the instructions sent out to the company's agents in Russia in 1557.[7] Barne also imported wine from Spain, where his son Philip was acting as his factor in 1538,[8] and exported cloth.[9] He was a promoter of the Guinea voyages of 1553 and 1554.[10] During his lifetime Barne had been associated with Henry Becher, Sir John Gresham, and others in buying property in London,[11] and on his death he left property there and in Herts to his widow Alice for life, with reversion to his sons, George and John.[12] George was later a governor of the Russia Company.[13]

Richard Barne. There were two merchants of this name, neither of whom seems to have been related to Sir George Barne and either of whom may have been the charter member. They were Richard Barne, merchant of the staple, who was exporting wool in 1554–5 and who died before the

---

[1] The name is also spelt Barnes, but Barne seems the more correct form.

[2] Hasted, p. 160.

[3] *C.P.R. 1548–9*, p. 152.   Barne left £10 to a married sister, Alice Kyngesbury of Wells.

[4] Beaven, ii. 31.   [5] Stow, *Annales*, ed. 1631, p. 609.

[6] J. Robertson, 'The first Russian embassy to England ', *Archaeological Journal*, xiii. 77–8.

[7] Hakluyt, i. 380–91.

[8] Marsden, i. 61, 72, 106–10, 195.   Philip seems to have predeceased his father.

[9] Exch. K.R. Customs Accounts, 87/4, 167/1.

[10] Hakluyt, iv. 47 ; Williamson, *Sir John Hawkins*, p. 40.

[11] *C.P.R. 1548–9*, pp. 76–7 ; *1550–3*, pp. 133–5.

[12] P.C.C. 13 Noodes.   Alice died in 1559 (Strype, *Annals*, i. pt. 1. 286).

[13] S.P.D. Eliz., ccxxxviii, no. 129 ; *C.S.P.D. 1591–4*, p. 170 ; *C.S.P.For. 1584–5*, pp. 132, 222.

end of 1588,[1] and Richard Barne, mercer and merchant adventurer in 1559, who died in 1597 or 1598.[2]

Francis Barnham. He was the son of Stephen Barnham of Southwick, Hants,[3] and entered the Drapers Company by apprenticeship in 1541 [4] and was master in 1569 and 1571.[5] He was an alderman from 1568 until his death in May 1576.[6] Barnham was an assistant of the Russia Company in 1569,[7] but he does not seem to have been actively engaged in other branches of foreign trade. His bequest of £4 to the clothiers of Guildford and Basingstoke for a dinner suggests that he was engaged in the cloth trade, but he was not apparently a cloth exporter. Barnham was a wealthy man, lending to the crown in 1569 [8] and leaving land and houses in London, Surrey, Essex, and Wales as well as personal property worth more than £2200. Most of his estate went to his wife, Alice, and to his youngest son, Benedict.[9] Benedict himself left a personal estate of £14,614.[10]

Humphrey Baskerfeld. Baskerfeld was born at Wolverley in Worcestershire [11] and died a well-to-do London merchant. He was a member of the Mercers Company and its master in 1560. He was an alderman from 1558 until his death in February 1564.[12] His trade seems to have been chiefly in cloth [13] and he is said to have been one of the leading merchant adventurers.[14] At his death Baskerfeld left personal property worth more than £7000, of which one-third went to his widow Jane, the daughter of Humphrey Packington, who later married Sir Lionel Duckett, and one-third to four daughters, two sons, and a child unborn, each of whom was to receive £200 in addition to his or her child's portion. He also left £200 to the Mercers Company and loans of £100 for one year to each of two clothiers, Thomas Clarke the younger of Coggeshall and Thomas Dodinge of Worcester.[15]

---

[1] Exch. K.R. Customs Accounts, 87/7 ; *A.P.C. 1588*, pp. 424–5.

[2] *C.P.R. 1558–60*, p. 200 ; P.C.C. 29 Lewyn.

[3] Overall, p. 80 n.   [4] Boyd, p. 12.   [5] Johnson, ii. 471.

[6] Beaven, ii. 38.   [7] Hakluyt, ii. 86.

[8] Strype, i. bk. i. 283. Sir Ralph Bagnall owed Barnham £1000 in 1565 and had owed and repaid him £700 the year before (*C.S.P.D. 1601–3, Add. 1547–65*, p. 557).

[9] P.C.C. 10 Carew. In his will he left £100 to the Drapers Company for loans to young men, but a codicil revoked this. His son Benedict was a benefactor of St. Alban's Hall, Oxford, and father in law of Francis Bacon (*D.N.B.*).

[10] Common Serjeant's Book, i. f. 98 (Corporation of London Records Office).   [11] P.C.C. 9 Stevenson.   [12] Beaven, ii. 36.

[13] Exch. K.R. Customs Accounts, 86/6, 167/1 ; S.P.D. Eliz., vi. no. 52.

[14] Burgon, i. 259.

[15] P.C.C. 9 Stevenson ; Overall, p. 37 n.

Henry Becher. According to the rather curious statement in the Herald's Visitation of Bedfordshire in 1634 Becher was ' yongest of eleven sons, and was heire to all their lands which they had in gavel kind in Kent '.[1] He was certainly a citizen, haberdasher, merchant, and merchant adventurer of London [2] and an alderman from 1567 to 1571.[3] He was a charter assistant of the Russia Company and a consul in 1569.[4] He was also a charter assistant of the Merchant Adventurers' Company in 1564.[5] In the 'fifties and 'sixties Becher was engaged in extensive foreign trade. He was a promoter of the Guinea voyage of 1558.[6] He exported cloth to Antwerp, from which he imported miscellaneous goods including paper, pins, and cloves.[7] He imported sugar from Barbary [8] and was engaged in the silk trade.[9] He also provided costly imported fabrics for the court entertainments.[10] Whether it was from his inheritance, his trade, or his numerous deals in real property,[11] he died on 15 January 1571 a prosperous man, who could begin his will with the rather nonchalant statement that he did not owe above £400. He left houses and land in London and in nine counties and disposed of his third of the personal property in bequests which exceeded £2000.[12]

John, earl of Bedford, lord keeper of the Privy Seal.[13]

William Billingsley.
He was a haberdasher and one of the assay masters of the Mint.[14]

Sir Richard Blount, knight.
Blount was appointed master of the Ordnance at Calais in 1546 [15] and was later a gentleman of the Privy Chamber

---

[1] F. A. Page Turner, ' The Becher family of Howbury ', *Beds. Historical Record Society*, v. 133–62. This article gives an account of Becher's children, one of whom, William, married Judith, daughter of John Quarles.

[2] *C.P.R. 1558–60*, p. 169.

[3] Beaven, ii. 38.   [4] Hakluyt, ii. 86.

[5] Patent Rolls, 6 Eliz., pt. 12. Lingelbach, *The Merchant Adventurers of England*, pp. 231–2, gives the name as Beechat and Preacher.

[6] H.C.A. Libels, 37. no. 247.

[7] Exch. K.R. Customs Accounts, 87/4, 167/1 ; Exch. K.R. Port Books, 2/1, 4/2.   [8] Exch. K.R. Port Books, 3/2.   [9] S.P.D. Eliz., xx. no. 63.

[10] Feuillerat, *Documents relating to the office of the revels in the time of Queen Elizabeth*, pp. 82, 87, 93, 99.

[11] *C.P.R. 1550–3*, p. 244 ; *1553–4*, pp. 334–5 ; *1557–8*, pp. 123–4.

[12] P.C.C. 10 Holney ; *Inq. p.m. Lond.*, ii. 150–3.

[13] *D.N.B.*, John Russell, first earl of Bedford, 1486?–1555.

[14] *C.P.R. 1550–3*, p. 301 ; *Letters and Papers, Henry VIII*, xx. pt. i. 302 ; R. Ruding, *Annals of the coinage*, i. 91, 107.

[15] *Letters and Papers, Henry VIII*, xxi. pt. ii. 231.

and lieutenant of the Tower.[1] On 17 October 1552 he was appointed collector of the great and petty custom and subsidy of Southampton.[2] In 1553 he was M.P. for Steyning and in 1563 for Oxfordshire.[3] He lived at Mapledurham, Oxfordshire, and died in 1564 leaving property in Sussex, Oxon, Bucks, Middlesex, Devon, and Somerset.[4]

Philip Bold. He was a clothworker, a merchant adventurer exporting cloth to Antwerp,[5] and M.P. for London in 1555.[6] With Thomas Cecil he paid £1775 for chantry lands in 1552, and in 1556 was selling former chantry property in Wolverhampton to Thomas Offley and three years later houses in London to Miles Mording.[7] In 1559 Bold was described as 'late of London, merchant, alias of Aldenham, co. Herts'.[8]

William Bond. Bond was a haberdasher, an alderman from 1567 to 1576,[9] and 'a Merchant Adventurer, and most famous (in his age) for his great adventures both by sea and land'.[10] He was a shipowner,[11] an exporter of cloth to Antwerp, and an importer of wine from France.[12] He probably traded with Spain [13] and certainly traded with the Baltic, where his trade with Narva brought him into conflict with the Russia Company. After the capture of Narva by the Russians in 1558, the company claimed that it came within their monopoly area and tried to stop Bond and others from trading there. In 1564 Bond was imprisoned in the Fleet for a week for disobeying the Privy Council's order to cease trade with Narva [14] and two years later the company's monopoly of the Narva trade was confirmed by statute.[15] Despite this, Bond prospered. He bought Crosby Place for a residence in 1567 [16] and lent £1500 to the crown in 1569 [17] and gave his daughter a dowry of £1000. He died on 31 May 1576, leaving Crosby Place and six messuages in London and a personal estate worth at least £4200.[18] His brother, Sir George Bond, who died in 1592, left a personal estate of £8127.[19]

---

[1] Strype, i. bk. i. 69. [2] *C.P.R. 1553*, p. 380.
[3] *Return*, i. 380, 405. [4] P.C.C. 25 Stevenson.
[5] Exch. K.R. Customs Accounts, 167/1 ; Burgon, i. 466 ; Smit, i. 757.
[6] *Return*, i. 393.
[7] *C.P.R. 1550–3*, pp. 441–4 ; *1555–7*, p. 207 ; *1558–60*, p. 132.
[8] Ibid., *1558–60*, p. 213.
[9] Beaven, ii. 38. [10] Strype, i. bk. ii. 101.
[11] Oppenheim, *A history of the administration of the royal navy*, pp. 179–80.
[12] Exch. K.R. Port Books, 2/1, 4/2.
[13] *C.S.P. For. 1572–4*, p. 589.
[14] S.P.D. Eliz., xxxv. nos. 20–3 ; *A.P.C. 1558–70*, pp. 160, 163, 178–80.
[15] Hakluyt, ii. 66–72. [16] Beaven, ii. 173. [17] Burgon, ii. 342.
[18] P.C.C. 26 Carew ; *Inq. p.m. Lond.*, ii. 199–201.
[19] Common Serjeant's Book, i. f. 57 (Corporation of London Records Office).

Stephen Borough.[1]   Borough was master of the *Edward Bonaventure* in the voyage of 1553 and was subsequently master of other ships making the voyage to St. Nicholas.   The account of his life in the *D.N.B.* divides his career into two parts, ' the first as servant to the merchant adventurers trading to Russia, the second as servant to the queen '.   It assumes that his last voyage to Russia was made in 1561, and that this voyage marked the end of the first part of his career.   These assumptions are unfounded.   Stephen Borough was a shipmaster on the voyage to Russia in 1564,[2] 1565,[3] and 1567.[4]   He went to Russia again in 1568,[5] presumably as a shipmaster.   Finally in 1571 he made what seems to be his last recorded voyage to Russia as a shipmaster.[6]   In 1574 Borough was one of the Russia Company's representatives at a conference with Frobisher over the north-west passage.[7]

Sir John Bourne, knight and principal secretary.   He was M.P. for Worcestershire in 1554, 1555, and 1558 [8] and owned property in that county.[9]   He received an annuity of £100 in 1558 on surrendering his office of secretary.[10]

John Branche.   He was born about 1515, the son of John Branche, draper of London,[11] and became free of the Drapers Company by apprenticeship in 1539.[12]   Later he was four times master of the Drapers.[13]   For some reason Branche tried to avoid serving as alderman and sheriff in 1570,[14] but he was elected for both offices and was mayor in 1580-1 when he was knighted.[15] He secured his discharge from the aldermanry in 1586 on the grounds of ' age, weakness, and other infirmityes of body ' and died two years later.[16]   He was a cloth exporter [17] and ' of great wealth in land and goods '.[18]   Some of his wealth probably came from his second wife, Ellen the widow of John Minors, for Minors had been both rich and childless.[19]   Branche maintained a house

---

[1] *D.N.B.*, Stephen Borough, 1525–84.   The statement in *D.N.B.* that Borough was made chief pilot of England seems to be incorrect.   Oppenheim, op. cit., p. 149, shows that the proposal to make him chief pilot was never carried out.

[2] Exch. K.R. Customs Accounts, 90/11.

[3] Exch. K.R. Port Books, 2/1.

[4] Ibid., 4/2 ; Johnson, ii. 456.

[5] Lans. MSS. 11, no. 37 ; Morgan and Coote, ii. 256–7, 261.

[6] Exch. K.R. Port Books, 5/1.

[7] R. Collinson, *The three voyages of Martin Frobisher*, p. 89.

[8] *Return*, i. 388, 395, 399.

[9] P.C.C. 29 Pyckering.   [10] *C.P.R. 1557–8*, p. 100.

[11] J. J. Baddeley, *Aldermen of Cripplegate Ward*, pp. 51–2.

[12] Boyd, p. 25.   [13] Johnson, ii. 471–2.   [14] Overall, p. 124 n.

[15] Beaven, ii. 39.   [16] Baddeley, op. cit., pp. 51–2.

[17] S.P.D. Eliz., vi. no. 52.   [18] Strype, ii. bk. v. 156–7.   [19] Ibid.

in London in ' Grene Lettyce Lane ' and in Essex called Garnish Hall. He died without issue leaving property in London which included ' the Ould Muscovye House '.[1]

John Broke. Broke, who was a member of the Drapers Company, was both a charter member and an employee of the Russia Company. He may have been sent out as a factor to Vardö in 1555 [2] and he was certainly the company's London agent between 1565 and 1569.[3] When he ceased to be agent the company claimed that he owed it £851 1s. 3d. for ready money and merchandise ' which he tooke out of their accountes ' and £250 for calls on his stock which he had not met. Broke was imprisoned ' above fifteen monthes ' for this debt.[4] It is not clear how the matter ended, but in 1580 Broke seems to have been elected renter of the Drapers Company.[5] Apart from his activities as an employee of the Russia Company, Broke was engaged in the wine trade with France in 1563 [6] and was a promoter of the Guinea voyage of 1558.[7]

Robert and Thomas Brown. It is impossible to identify the Browns.[8] The most prominent Robert Brown was a goldsmith and cloth exporter who died in 1575. He had both a brother and a son named Thomas.[9]

Henry Brunker, esquire. Henry Brunker ' of Erlestoke, Wilts, alias of Melksham, Wilts.',[10] was the son of Robert Brunker of Devizes.[11] He died in 1568 owning manors in fee simple worth £240 2s. 10d. p.a. He left this property to his two sons, Henry and William, and his ' stocke of monye ' in the Russia Company to the elder son, Henry.[12]

John Buckland. Buckland, who may have been a Devon man,[13] was mate of the *Edward Bonaventure* on the voyage to Russia in 1553 and master of that ship on the voyage of 1555. He survived the wreck of the ship on its return in 1556, for he was master of the *Primrose* in the Russian voyage of 1557.[14]

---

[1] P.C.C. 55 Rutland ; *Inq. p.m. Lond.*, iii. 133–4.
[2] Hakluyt, i. 303–4.   [3] Exch. K.R. Port Books, 2/1, 4/2.
[4] S.P.D. Eliz., cviii. nos. 62–3.   [5] Johnson, i. 177.
[6] H.C.A. Examinations, 15 (3 Aug., 2 Oct. 1564).
[7] H.C.A. Libels, 37. no. 247.
[8] On the difficulty of distinguishing the Browns at this period, see *Notes and Queries*, 7th series, v. 151–3.
[9] Exch. K.R. Port Books, 2/1 ; P.C.C. 26 Pyckering ; *C.P.R. 1553–4*, p. 493.   [10] *C.P.R. 1558–60*, p. 152.
[11] *Letters and Papers, Henry VIII*, xv. 167.   [12] P.C.C. 15 Babington.
[13] *C.P.R. 1550–3*, p. 83.   [14] Hakluyt, i. 241, 245, 303, 357, 381.

William Bulley. Bulley who was born at Bacton, Norfolk, about 1508[1] was a fishmonger, a cloth exporter,[2] and owner of the *Marten Bulley* in 1545 and part owner of the *White Hind* in 1546. Both ships were engaged in privateering.[3] He was an assistant of the Russia Company in 1569[4] and died in 1575 leaving a wharf and quay to his wife Mary for life with reversion to his four sons.[5]

George Burton. He went out to Russia in the *Edward Bonaventure* in 1553 as cape merchant.[6]

Nicholas Burton. He may have been the cape merchant of that name who was loading the *Lion* in Spain in 1561 when he was seized and imprisoned by the Inquisition for allowing the master and mariners ' to labor uppon the holye dayes '.[7]

Sebastian Cabot, esquire.[8] Cabot drew up the ordinances for the first voyage to Russia in 1553[9] and was appointed governor of the company for life in the charter of 1555. Beazley assumed that Cabot was dismissed from the governorship and that by 21 February 1557 his place had been taken by Anthony Hussey.[10] This seems doubtful. Hussey was then governor of the Merchant Adventurers' Company and Beazley appears to have confused the two companies. Moreover on 16 May 1557 a cargo, which included wax, was entered by the customs in Cabot's name.[11] This was probably the cargo of the *Philip and Mary* which arrived from Russia on 18 April 1557.[12] This suggests that Cabot was still governor, though later such cargoes were entered in the name of the London agent of the company. Cabot seems to have died in the last quarter of 1557.[13] The fact that Robert Record dedicated *The Whetstone of Witte* to the governors of the company in November 1557,[14] suggests that Cabot was then dead.

---

[1] H.C.A. Examinations, 12 (29 June 1558).

[2] Exch. K.R. Customs Accounts, 87/4.

[3] *A.P.C. 1542–7*, pp. 374, 376, 410 ; Marsden, i. 139–41.

[4] Hakluyt, ii. 86.   [5] P.C.C. 38 Pyckering.

[6] Hakluyt, i. 241, 245.

[7] H.C.A. Examinations, 14 (17, 22 Nov. 1561).

[8] *D.N.B.*, Sebastian Cabot, 1474–1557.

[9] Hakluyt, i. 232–41.

[10] C. R. Beazley, *John and Sebastian Cabot*, p. 202.

[11] Exch. K.R. Customs Accounts, 86/6.

[12] Hakluyt, i. 358.

[13] J. A. Williamson, *The voyages of the Cabots*, p. 284.

[14] E. G. R. Taylor, *Tudor geography*, p. 24.

July Campeney.

Alexander Carleill. Carleill married Anne, daughter of Sir George Barne, by whom he had two children, Christopher, a naval and military commander,[1] and Alice, who married Christopher Hoddesdon,[2] a former apprentice of Sir George Barne and later an agent[3] and a member of the Russia Company.[4] Carleill was a member of the Vintners Company and one time its master.[5] He was a wine importer.[6] He died in 1561 leaving the Sarazen's Head in Bagshot and a house in London to his wife with reversion to his son Christopher.[7] His widow married Sir Francis Walsingham.

George Cassie. He was a cloth exporter in 1553–4.[8]

Edward Castelin. The Castelins appear to have been a Derbyshire family,[9] of whom two members, William and James, were trading with Italy, the Levant, Spain, Portugal, and the Azores in 1528–30.[10] Edward Castelin traded with the Canaries[11] and was a promoter of the Guinea voyages of 1554, 1558, 1561, 1563, and 1564.[12] and of Hawkins's second slaving voyage.[13] He was a shipowner,[14] a cloth exporter,[15] a member of the Merchant Adventurers' Company,[16] and a charter member of the Mineral and Battery Works.[17] In 1576 Castelin was in Germany trying to raise a loan for the Queen, but the results seem to have been meagre.[18] Other members of the family traded

---

[1] *D.N.B.*, Christopher Carleill, 1551?–1593, where it is said that Christopher married Mary, daughter of Sir Francis Walsingham, who in fact died unmarried in 1580, aged about 7 (C. Read, *Mr. Secretary Walsingham and the policy of Queen Elizabeth*, iii. 425).

[2] *D.N.B.*, Sir Christopher Hoddesdon, 1534–1611.

[3] *H.M.C. Pepys*, p. 143.

[4] D. B. Quinn, *The voyages and colonising enterprises of Sir Humphrey Gilbert*, i. 76–80, ii. 365–9.

[5] Machyn, p. 269.   [6] Exch. K.R. Customs Accounts, 86/6.

[7] P.C.C. 31 Loftes.   [8] Exch. K.R. Customs Accounts, 87/4.

[9] S. O. Addy, 'Wills at Somerset House relating to Derbyshire', *Journal of the Derbyshire Arch. and Natural History Society*, xlv. 75.

[10] Blake, ii. 415 n.

[11] L. de Alberti and A. B. W. Chapman, 'English traders and the Spanish Inquisition in the Canaries', *T.R.H.S.*, 3rd series, iii. 237–53.

[12] Hakluyt, iv. 47, 130–1, 133, 137 ; H.C.A. Libels, 37. no. 247.

[13] Williamson, *Sir John Hawkins*, p. 92.

[14] Hakluyt, i. 380–1 ; Oppenheim, *Administration of the royal navy*, pp. 122–3.

[15] Exch. K.R. Customs Accounts, 87/4.

[16] Patent Rolls, 6 Eliz., pt. 12.   [17] Carr, p. 19.

[18] *C.S.P. For. 1575–7*, pp. 339, 358 ; F. C. Dietz, *English public finance, 1558–1641*, p. 38.

with Spain [1] and a John Castelin was a member of the Russia Company in 1583.[2]

Thomas Castell. Castell became a member of the Drapers Company by apprenticeship in 1544 [3] and seems to have begun his commercial career by acting as a factor in Cadiz for Henry Richards.[4] Later he engaged in marine insurance [5] and was exporting cloth and importing raisins and canvas in 1553–4 and importing oil in 1556–7, apparently in partnership with Thomas Chamber.[6] He died about 1559.[7] His wife was Richard Duckett's sister.[8]

Sir William Cecil, knight.[9] Cecil paid the initial 'subscription' of £25 to the Russia Company and paid a further £75 in calls by March 1557.[10] He held stock in the company in 1568 [11] and in 1595 was described as 'the most ancient person living of all the same company'.[12]

Thomas Chamber. He was probably the London grocer of that name who was exporting cloth in 1553–4,[13] supplying Danzig cordage for the navy in 1557–8,[14] and was apparently engaged in marine insurance with Thomas Castell in 1548 and with Castell and Robert Dove in 1559.[15]

Richard Chamberlain. Chamberlain was a prominent member of the Ironmongers Company of which he was master in 1560 and 1565 and to which he left £50.[16] He was an alderman from 1560 until his death on 19 November 1566.[17] His epitaph describes him as ' Merchant Adventurer, and free of Russia '.[18] He was a charter assistant of the Russia Company and a charter member of the Merchant Adventurers in 1564.[19] Chamberlain's chief trade seems to have been in cloth to Antwerp, but he also exported

---

[1] Patent Rolls, 19 Eliz., pt. 8.

[2] Quinn, *Voyages and colonising enterprises of Sir Humphrey Gilbert*, i. 76–80.

[3] Boyd, p. 35.   [4] Marsden, i. 126.   [5] Ibid., ii. 46, 51.

[6] Exch. K.R. Customs Accounts, 86/2, 6, 87/4 ; H.C.A. Examinations, 14 (7 June 1561).

[7] Boyd, p. 35. His daughter Alice married Henry Hawarde and their son John was the reporter of the Star Chamber cases (*Les Reportes del Cases in Camera Stellata*, ed. W. P. Baildon, pp. xiv–xv).

[8] P.C.C. 48 Wrastley.

[9] *D.N.B.*, William Cecil, baron Burghley, 1520–98.

[10] Lans. MSS. 118, f. 52.

[11] *C.S.P. For. 1566–8*, p. 463.   [12] *H.M.C. Salisbury*, v. 462.

[13] *C.P.R. 1558–60*, p. 206 ; Exch. K.R. Customs Accounts, 87/4.

[14] Harl. MSS. 253, f. 18d.   [15] Marsden, ii. 46, 51.

[16] Nicholl, p. 545 ; P.C.C. 7 Stonarde.   [17] Beaven, ii. 36.

[18] Strype, i. bk. iii. 55–6.   [19] Patent Rolls, 6 Eliz., pt. 12.

cloth to Spain.[1] He was a wealthy man, living in a ' great messuage or mansion house ' he built in Old Jewry, and inheriting a life interest in much London property from his first wife, Anne, the daughter of Robert Downe. Of the eight sons born to this marriage one was John Chamberlain, the letter writer, who was aged 13 at his father's death and who having ' ben tendre, sicklye, and weake ', was to be ' broughte up to learning ' under the care of Thomas Gore, grocer.[2] The eldest son, Robert, seems to have been a member of the Russia Company in 1598 and its governor in 1604.[3] Chamberlain's second wife was Margaret, daughter of Nicholas Hurleton of Cheshire and widow of a London grocer.[4] Chamberlain left her £2200,[5] but despite this legacy she seems to have carried on in trade.[6]

Richard Chancellor.[7]

William Chester, alderman.[8] The account of Chester in the *D.N.B.* does not say much about his trading activities and its statement that he was ' very successful in the eastern trade ' seems based entirely on the fact that he was a member of the Russia Company when it was trading through Russia to Persia. Chester was a merchant of the staple, exporting wool to Calais in 1554-5, and was mayor of the staple in 1552 and 1561.[9] He was a merchant adventurer exporting cloth [10] and he traded with France [11] and Barbary.[12] He was a promoter of the Guinea voyages of the fifteen-fifties and fifteen-sixties and of the slaving voyage of 1564.[13] Chester was part owner of ships engaged in the Russia and Guinea trades [14] and was a prominent member of the Russia Company, of which he was governor in 1567 [15] and probably in 1569 [16] and

---

[1] S.P.D. Eliz., vi. no. 52 ; Exch. K.R. Port Books, 2/1 ; Exch. K.R. Customs Accounts, 87/4, 167/1.

[2] P.C.C. F 2 Wrastley, 7 Stonarde ; *Inq. p.m. Lond.*, i. 158–60 ; N. E. McClure, *The letters of John Chamberlain*, i. 2–3.   [3] S.P. Foreign Russia, i. ff. 118, 194.

[4] Machyn, p. 391.   [5] P.C.C. 7 Stonarde.

[6] Exch. K.R. Port Books, 4/2, 6/3. She imported sugar from Barbary, a branch of trade in which Thomas Gore was active.

[7] *D.N.B.*, Richard Chancellor, d. 1556.

[8] *D.N.B.*, Sir William Chester, 1509?–1595?.

[9] Exch. K.R. Customs Accounts, 87/7 ; *C.P.R. 1550–3*, p. 228 ; A. L. Jenckes, *The origin, the organisation, and location of the Staple*, p. 67.

[10] Exch. K.R. Customs Accounts, 87/4, 167/1 ; S.P.D. Eliz., vi. no. 52 ; Patent Rolls, 8 Eliz., pt. 12.

[11] Smit, ii. 898.   [12] *C.S.P.D. 1547–80*, p. 183.

[13] H.C.A. Libels, 37. no. 247 ; Hakluyt, iv. 133, 137 ; Williamson, *Sir John Hawkins*, pp. 54, 92.

[14] Hakluyt, i. 380–1 ; Williamson, op. cit., pp. 114, 162.

[15] Hakluyt, ii. 50–1.   [16] Lans. MSS. 11, no. 37.

1570.[1] It is usually assumed that Chester died about 1595, but in 1574 the Drapers Company wrote to the governor of the Merchant Adventurers ' in favour of J. Northen, sometime apprentice to Sir William Chester, his master being departed this life before his coming out of Russia '.[2] As John Northen or Norton was in Russia in the summer of 1572,[3] it would appear that Chester died sometime between then and 1574. He seems to have been a rich man for his wealth was variously estimated at between £7000 and £15000 in 1559.[4]

Sir John Clere, knight. Clere was a Norfolk landowner, a naval commander,[5] and M.P. for Bramber in 1542, Thetford in 1553, and Norfolk in 1555.[6] He died in 1557.[7]

Clement Clerke. He was probably a draper, a merchant of the staple, and a cloth exporter.[8] If he is to be identified with the Clement Clerke of Bocking, Essex, who died in 1562, he owned two houses in London and farms and tenements in Essex.[9]

William Clifton, esquire. Clifton, who was a charter assistant of the Russia Company, seems to have been a merchant tailor.[10] He was connected with the customs service in 1546 [11] and in the following year he and Sir Anthony Dennye were granted the office of collector of the subsidies of tonnage and poundage in the port of London and of keeper and governor of the seal called ' cokett ' in that port.[12] In 1552 Clifton bought the manor of Barrington, Somerset, from Henry, duke of Suffolk, and Thomas Duport,[13] and later in the 'fifties he was buying manors in Somerset and Devon in company with Humphrey Colles and Lionel Duckett.[14] He was also a partner with Duckett in a licence and stock of £750 for buying and selling felts.[15] By 1559 Clifton seems to have retired to Somerset [16] and his will of 20 July 1562 describes him as of Barrington in that county. He left his share of one-tenth in the felt licence and stock to his son-in-law Miles Sandes of the Middle Temple and

---

[1] Morgan and Coote, ii. 296.   [2] Johnson, ii. 457.

[4] Hakluyt, ii. 156.

[5] H.C.A. Examinations, 12 (30 Jan., 1 Feb. 1559).

[3] *Letters and Papers, Henry VIII*, xxi. pt. i. 234 ; *A.P.C. 1556–8*, pp. 120, 139, 141.   [6] *Return*, i. 373, 379, 394.   [7] P.C.C. 34 Wrastley.

[8] Johnson, ii. 405, 407 ; *C.P.R. 1557–8*, p. 301 ; Exch. K.R. Customs Accounts, 167/1.   [9] P.C.C. 9 Streat.   [10] Clode, ii. 341.

[11] G. Schanz, *Englische Handelspolitik*, ii. 371.

[12] *C.P.R. 1547–8*, p. 19.   [13] *Ibid. 1550–3*, p. 416.

[14] *Ibid. 1555–7*, pp. 93, 345.   [15] P.C.C. 34 Stevenson.

[16] *C.P.R. 1558–60*, p. 236.

his stock in the Russia Company to his two sons and three daughters equally. If all these children died without issue, then £400 was to be used for establishing a free school at Barrington.[1]

Thomas Colshill, gentleman. Colshill was appointed supervisor of the petty custom and subsidy for London in 1549,[2] though later he was said to be 'an odd man for a Surveyor, which overlooketh all the rest'.[3] The volume of statistics on English merchant shipping in 1572 was his work.[4] He seems to have been M.P. for Knaresboro' in 1558 and for Aylesbury in 1563.[5] He was buying and selling land in Hackney between 1547 and 1550 [6] and in 1560 bought land in Somerset in company with Thomas Lodge, Lionel Duckett, William Clifton's son-in-law, Miles Sandes, and others.[7]

William Cordell, esquire, solicitor general.[8]

John Cotton. A John Cotton was a merchant of the staple in 1558.[9]

John Crymes. He was probably the John Crymes, clothworker, who paid £757 for land in Staffordshire in 1546 [10] and who three years later bought, in company with Nicholas Bacon, houses in London and two-thirds of a 'salte house' in Northwich for £391.[11] He died on 14 July 1555 leaving property in London and Staffordshire worth £66 4s. 8d. p.a.[12]

Thomas Curtes, alderman. He was the son of John Curtes of Enfield, Middlesex,[13] and was a prominent member of the Pewterers Company, of which he was four times master.[14] Curtes tried to refuse the office of sheriff in 1546, 'declaring his inhabilitie of substance', but at last 'with an evill will he tooke his oth'.[15] Similarly on his election as alderman in 1551 he resisted for some years that transfer to one of the twelve great livery companies which custom demanded. Only after a fine of 100 marks and committal to

---

[1] P.C.C. 34 Stevenson.   [2] *C.P.R. 1549–51*, p. 65.
[3] Strype, i. bk. ii. 51.   [4] *C.S.P.D. Add. 1566–79*, pp. 440–1.
[5] *Return*, i. 399, 403.
[6] *C.P.R. 1547–8*, p. 213 ; *1548–9*, p. 84 ; *1549–51*, p. 358.
[7] Ibid. *1558–60*, p. 381.
[8] *D.N.B.*, Sir William Cordell, d. 1581. Cordell bequeathed to Burghley a parchment book containing a matter between Henry VII and Edmund Dudley, which was in the bottom of a chest in his study in the Rolls (P.C.C. 42 Darcy).
[9] *C.P.R. 1557–8*, p. 301.
[10] *Letters and Papers, Henry VIII*, xxi. pt. i. 579.
[11] *C.P.R. 1548–9*, p. 16.   [12] *Inq. p.m. Lond.*, i. 147–8.
[13] Herbert, *Livery companies*, ii. 43 n.   [14] Beaven, ii. 33.
[15] C. Wriothesley, *A Chronicle of England* (Camden Society, N.S., xi), i. 171.

Newgate did he transfer to the Fishmongers.[1] He was mayor in 1557-8 when he was knighted and was M.P. for London from 1547 to 1551. He died on 27 November 1559.[2] There seems little trace of Curtes's commercial activities, though he was trading with Chios sometime between 1533 and 1544.[3] He left property in London worth £155 13s. 4d. p.a. and in Essex value £12 p.a. The property went to Anne, the daughter of his late son Thomas.[4] Anne married Thomas Stukeley who was reported to be busy in the midst of Curtes's coffers before Curtes had been buried.[5]

Sir William Dansell, knight. Dansell was receiver general of the Court of Wards and Liveries [6] and royal agent at Antwerp in 1550.[7] He was removed from the latter office in April 1551 ' by reason of his slacknes ' and was succeeded by Sir Thomas Gresham.[8] He was governor of the Merchant Adventurers in 1552 [9] and M.P. for Arundel in 1555.[10] Dansell died in 1582 leaving £100 to Oxford University and £200 to the Mercers Company from which an annuity of £12 was to be paid to Anne Watkyns, his ' supposed base daughter '. His bequests to servants ranged from £1 to Robert Moinford, his boy in the kitchen, to £60 to James Scrobye, yeoman, who also received £40 for acting as an executor.[11]

Thomas, lord Darcy. Thomas Darcy was born in 1506 and knighted in 1532.[12] He was a gentleman of the Privy Chamber under Henry VIII and Edward VI, when he was buying much property from the crown.[13] In 1547 Darcy owned the *James*, a ship engaged in the Iceland fishing,[14] and was granted a licence to export wheat, beer, tanned leather, and calf skins.[15] In the same year he was M.P. for Essex.[16] He was created baron Darcy of Chiche, Essex, in 1551 and died in 1558, leaving property in Essex to his wife and sons.[17]

Christopher Dauntsey. Dauntsey was a mercer and a cloth exporter in 1547.[18] On Mary's accession he replaced Thomas Gresham as royal agent

---

[1] C. Welsh, *History of the worshipful company of Pewterers*, ii. 218 ; Baddeley, *Aldermen of Cripplegate Ward*, pp. 145-7.

[2] Beaven, ii. 33.   [3] Hakluyt, iii. 6.
[4] *Inq. p.m. Lond.*, i. 210-11.   [5] *C.S.P. For. 1559-60*, p. 138.
[6] *C.P.R., 1549-50*, p. 311.   [7] *C.S.P. Spanish, 1550-2*, p. 79.
[8] *D.N.B.*, art. Sir Thomas Gresham.   [9] *A.P.C. 1550-2*, p. 501.
[10] *Return*, i. 394.   [11] P.C.C. 34 Tirwhite.
[12] *Complete Peerage*, iv. 78.
[13] *Letters and Papers, Henry VIII*, xxi. pt. i. 764.
[14] Marsden, ii. 6-7.   [15] *Letters and Papers, Henry VIII*, xxi. pt. ii. 422.
[16] *Return*, i. 375.   [17] *Complete Peerage*, iv. 78 ; P.C.C. 10 Loftes.
[18] Exch. K.R. Customs Accounts, 167/1.

at Antwerp, but after borrowing at unnecessarily high rates of interest, he was removed from office in November 1553.[1] The following year Dauntsey received a licence to import felts or hats from Spain or Portugal for ten years, but he soon assigned the licence to Lionel Duckett and Henry Vinar.[2] At that time he was importing figs, probably from Spain.[3] In 1559 he seems to have been concerned in the victualling of Guernsey.[4]

Robert Dawbeney. Dawbeney was born at Sharrington, Norfolk,[5] and became a merchant tailor in London and master of the Merchant Tailors in 1544.[6] He died in 1558, leaving a house, shop, and cellars on Watling Street in Aldermary to his wife Elizabeth with reversion to his eldest son Arthur.[7] Arthur was a Barbary trader and later a member of the Spanish and Barbary Companies.[8]

William Dawkes. Dawkes was a mercer and exporter of cloth to Antwerp.[9] He died in August 1555 leaving pastures and a house in Worcestershire, a house in Bethnal Green, and personal property worth more than £1600. His bequests to the poor and for founding a free school at Droitwich, where his parents lived, suggest that he came from there.[10]

Robert Dove. Dove was born in 1523, the son of Henry Dove of Stradbrook, Suffolk, and was apprenticed to Nicholas Wilford, a London merchant tailor. He became free of the Merchant Tailors in 1550 and was later master of the company and one of its greatest benefactors. He died on 2 May 1612.[11] Dove was engaged in marine insurance[12] and was an exporter of cloth and an importer of wine and raisins.[13] He traded with the Baltic[14] and Spain[15] and was a member of the Spanish and Levant Companies.[16]

---

[1] Burgon, i. 128–9. *D.N.B.*, art. Sir Thomas Gresham confuses him with alderman William Dauntsey, who died in 1543 (Beaven, i. 168). de Roover, *Gresham on foreign exchange*, p. 19, repeats this error.

[2] *C.P.R. 1553–4*, p. 399 ; Chancery Proceedings, second series, 50. no. 93.

[3] Exch. K.R. Customs Accounts, 86/2.

[4] *C.P.R. 1558–60*, pp. 112–13.   [5] P.C.C. 57 Noodes.

[6] Clode, i. 340.   [7] P.C.C. 57 Noodes.

[8] Exch. K.R. Port Books, 2/1, 6/3 ; Patent Rolls, 19 Eliz., pt. 8 ; Hakluyt, iv. 268.   [9] Exch. K.R. Customs Accounts, 87/4, 167/1.

[10] P.C.C. F 31 More.

[11] Clode, i. 157–8. For details of his benefactions to the company, which totalled £3448, see Clode, *Memorials*, pp. 297–300.

[12] Marsden, ii. 51, 132.

[13] Exch. K.R. Customs Accounts, 86/2, 6, 87/4, 90/11.

[14] *C.P.R. 1560–3*, p. 8.   [15] Exch. K.R. Port Books, 2/1.

[16] Patent Rolls, 19 Eliz., pt. 8 ; Hakluyt, iii. 372 ; Carr, p. 31.

He seems to have been a member of the Russia Company until at least 1605.[1]

Robert Downe, the younger. He was presumably the son of Robert Downe,[2] a prominent member of the Ironmongers Company,[3] who died on 30 November 1556 leaving property in London value £74 13s. 4d. p.a. It is clear from the father's will, dated 4 August 1556,[4] and from the *inquisition post mortem*[5] that his son had predeceased him. The property was left to the elder Downe's daughter Anne and her husband Richard Chamberlain and their children.

Christopher Draper. He was the son of John Draper of Melton Mowbray[6] and was a member of the Ironmongers Company in 1537, of which he was later eight times master.[7] He was alderman, 1556–81, and mayor, 1566–7, when he was knighted ; he died 8 May 1581.[8] Of his three daughters, Bennet married Sir William Webbe, Agnes married Sir Wolstan Dixie, and Bridget married firstly Stephen Woodroff and secondly Sir Henry Billingsley.[9] Draper seems to have traded with Antwerp[10] and he was a member of the Spanish Company in 1577,[11] but his chief business was in supplying cables, cordage, and other material for the navy.[12] He also sold cables for the west country barges on the Thames[13] and supplied cordage for a ship making a voyage to Vardö in 1559.[14] In his will he left £20 for repairing and cleansing the Thames, £100 to the Ironmongers for loans, £60 for repairing roads, and two messuages in St. Dunstan in the East, one called ' the Gallie ' and the other ' Asheling Wharfe '.[15]

Lionel Duckett. Duckett was the son of William Duckett of Flintham, Notts, and was apprenticed to John Colet, a London mercer. He was

---

[1] S.P. Foreign Russia, i. f. 118 ; Hakluyt, ii. 355 ; S. Purchas, *Hakluytus Posthumus* (ed. 1905–7), xiv. 152, 168.

[2] S. Williams, *Letters written by John Chamberlain*, Camden Society, lxxix. pp. viii–x.

[3] Nicholl, pp. 446, 531–2.   [4] P.C.C. F 2 Wrastley.

[5] *Inq. p.m. Lond.*, i. 158–60.

[6] Machyn, p. 381. For pedigree see Hasted, p. 13, and *Collectanea Topographica*, iii. 150–1.

[7] Nicholl, pp. 59, 543.   [8] Beaven, ii. 35.

[9] Nicholl, p. 543. Beaven, ii. 172 wrongly states that Bridget married Nicholas Woodroff. Stephen and Nicholas were sons of David Woodroff.

[10] Smit, ii. 867 n.   [11] Patent Rolls, 19 Eliz., pt. 8.

[12] Harl. MSS. 253, f. 18d ; *A.P.C. 1547–50*, pp. 168, 232, 370 ; *1554–6*, p. 48.

[13] Marsden, ii. 139.   [14] H.C.A. Examinations, 17 (26 May 1569).

[15] P.C.C. 22 Darcy ; *Inq. p.m. Lond.*, iii. 36–7.

admitted to the freedom of the Mercers in 1537 [1] and was later four times master of the company. He was alderman from 1564 to 1587, mayor in 1572-3, when he was knighted, and he died in July 1587.[2] Duckett was twice married. His first wife was Mary, daughter of Hugh Leighton of Leighton, Salop, and his second Jane, daughter of Humphrey Packington and widow of Humphrey Baskerfeld.[3] Thomas, his son and heir by his second marriage, married Margaret [4] Nelson, a kinswoman of Duckett's servant, Thomas Nelson, and died without issue.

Duckett was a merchant adventurer, shipping cloth to Antwerp and importing wine.[5] He was a promoter of the Guinea voyage of 1558 and of the slaving voyages of 1562 to 1567 [6] and a member of the Spanish Company in 1577.[7] He held a share in a licence for importing felts.[8] All new ventures seem to have attracted Duckett, for he was a charter governor and very active member of the Mines Royal [9] and a subscriber to Frobisher's north-west voyages and one of the commissioners for winding up that unfortunate affair.[10] Undeterred by this experience, he became a charter member of Adrian Gilbert's Fellowship for the discovery of the north-west passage.[11] In addition Duckett was an active member of the Russia Company, of which he was an assistant in 1569 [12] and a governor in 1575 [13] and 1577.[14]

Duckett seems to have been a wealthy man. He was buying former monastic and chantry lands in Surrey, Staffs, and Derbyshire in 1553 [15] and lands in Somerset and Devon in 1556-7.[16] He lent £2000 to the crown in 1569.[17] He left property in Berkshire and a considerable personal estate.[18]

Richard Duckett. He was probably ' master Recherd Docket, grocer of London and marchand of Flanders ', who died 30 September 1557.[19] He seems to have been a cloth exporter,[20] and his will shows that he was in partnership

[1] Overall, p. 37 n.   [2] Beaven, ii. 37.   [3] Overall, p. 37 n.
[4] Overall, p. 37 n. calls her Mary, but she is given as Margaret in Duckett's will (P.C.C. 9 Rutland).
[5] Patent Rolls, 6 Eliz., pt. 12 ; Exch. K.R. Customs Accounts, 86/6, 87/4 ; S.P.D. Eliz., vi. no. 52 ; Smit, i. 707, ii. 822 ; Burgon, i. 259.
[6] Hakluyt, vii. 5 ; Williamson, *Sir John Hawkins*, p. 129 ; H.C.A. Libels, 37. no. 247.   [7] Patent Rolls, 19 Eliz., pt. 8.
[8] P.C.C. 34 Stevenson ; Chancery Proceedings, second series, 50. no. 93.
[9] Carr, p. 7 ; W. G. Collingwood, *Elizabethan Keswick*, pp. 35, 94, 176.
[10] *C.S.P. Colonial, East Indies, 1513–1616*, pp. 11, 18, 29, 37 ; *A.P.C. 1578–80*, p. 62.   [11] E. M. Tenison, *Elizabethan England*, v. 181.
[12] Hakluyt, ii. 86.   [13] H.C.A. Book of Acts, 16 (23 Feb. 1575).
[14] Carr, p. 28.   [15] *C.P.R. 1553*, pp. 233-4.
[16] Ibid. *1555–7*, pp. 93, 345.   [17] Strype, i. bk. i. 283 ; Burgon, ii. 343.
[18] P.C.C. 9 Rutland.   [19] Machyn, p. 154.
[20] Exch. K.R. Customs Accounts, 87/4, 167/1.

with another grocer, Francis Bowyer.[1] He left a gold ring to his master, Thomas Bowyer, which rather suggests that he may have gone into partnership with his master's son. He also left £13 6s. 8d. to his apprentice and brother-in-law, Edward Doughtie. Richard does not seem to have been related to Lionel Duckett, but he was related to the Drapers and the Castells.[2]

John Dymocke, esquire. Dymocke was born about 1493, the son of John Dymocke, citizen and draper of London,[3] and he entered the Drapers Company by redemption in 1529.[4] Under Henry VIII and Edward VI he was employed as a royal agent on the continent for buying provisions and levying soldiers.[5] While so engaged he made charges against Sir William Dansell for which he was committed to the Tower in 1552 and to the Fleet the following year.[6] Under Elizabeth, Dymocke was described as 'the queen's servant' and was apparently trying to sell jewels for her to the king of Sweden in 1561.[7] Later he was imprisoned in Sweden for his part in seizing for debts the goods of the king's sister, Cecilia of Baden, when she was in England in 1566.[8] Apart from his official duties, Dymocke was a cloth exporter [9] and owner and insurer of ships.[10] He resided in a house in Fenchurch Street where the Russian ambassador was lodged in 1557,[11] and 'lived 100 yeeres lacking 7 very commendably, and the 14th July 1585, he dyed Christianly'.[12]

Arthur Edwards. Edwards, who was a grocer, was an employee as well as a member of the Russia Company. He was sent out as a merchant on the *Edward Bonaventure* in 1553 and was in Russia in 1555 and 1557. Later he was employed in developing the trade with Persia through Russia, and he died at Astrakhan in 1580 while acting as one of the agents for the last Persian voyage.[13] He seems to have died without issue, leaving his

---

[1] P.C.C. 48 Wrastley.   [2] Ibid.   [3] Strype, i. bk. iii. 58.

[4] Boyd, p. 35.

[5] *A.P.C. 1542–7*, pp. 311, 490, 526 ; *1547–50*, p. 207 ; *C.S.P. For. 1547–53*, pp. 27–8.

[6] *A.P.C. 1550–2*, pp. 452, 473, 502 ; *1552–4*, pp. 280–1. The incident is obscure, but Dymocke was apparently involved in the internal politics of the Merchant Adventurers and was a leader of the New Hanse in its dispute with the Old Hanse.

[7] *C.P.R. 1558–60*, p. 334 ; *C.S.P. Spanish 1558–67*, p. 213.

[8] *C.S.P.D. 1547–80*, p. 468 ; *C.S.P. For. 1566–8*, pp. 102, 261 ; *1569–71*, p. 567 ; *1575–7*, p. 34.

[9] Exch. K.R. Customs Accounts, 87/4, 167/1.

[10] Hakluyt, i. 380–1 ; Marsden, ii. 46.

[11] Machyn, pp. 127, 130.   [12] Strype, i. bk. iii. 58.

[13] Hakluyt, i. 245, 308, 389 ; ii. 33–4, 108–9, 171–200.

' benefitte or freedome ' of the Russia Company to his cousin John Davenant.[1]
A ' Discourse towchinge Russia and Persia ' written in 1589 was based in
part on information which Edwards had supplied to the anonymous author.[2]

Thomas Egerton, esquire. Thomas Egerton, mercer, was ' treasurer
of the exchange of money ' under Edward VI and Mary [3] and was appointed
under treasurer of the exchange and Mint on 22 January 1554.[4] By 27 December 1555 he was ' late under-treasourer of the Mynte ' and was being called
to account for his employment of £20,000 ' of the Quenes Majesties treasure
in Spanishe money '.[5] Egerton seems to have misappropriated at least half of
this money, for which he was in prison in 1556, when he repaid £1020 10s.
and a further £640 realised by the sale of his house in London.[6] He seems to
have forfeited lands in Staffordshire because of this debt,[7] but it is not clear
how the matter ended or whether he was the same man as the Thomas Egerton
who was deputy governor of the Merchant Adventurers in 1575.[8]

John Eliot. He was a charter assistant of the Russia Company, but there
were too many merchants of that name for him to be identified. It is possible
that he was the John Eliot, mercer and cloth exporter, who was Thomas
Gresham's London factor in 1555.[9]

Richard Elkin.

Henry Fallowfield. Fallowfield was a shipowner [10] and an exporter of
cloth and importer of linen and canvas.[11] He lived at West Ham where he
died on 4 May 1566 aged 54 and was buried at Stratford Langton, ' a place
much frequented for the country houses of wealthy citizens, and the habita-
tions of such other of them who cannot enjoy their health in London '.[12]
Fallowfield left property in West Ham, London, and Oxfordshire and his
' adventure in Russia ' to his son Henry, and houses and land in Berks and
Bucks to his wife Mary with reversion to Henry. He also left his ship, with
the goods in it, to his wife and son, and £10 to his sister, Agnes Thornton,

---

[1] P.C.C. 4 Darcy. John Sparke, who witnessed Edwards's will, also left his
interest in the Russia Company to John Davenant, who was his son-in-law
(P.C.C. 5 Darcy).

[2] S.P.D. Eliz., ccxxiii. no. 52.   [3] *C.S.P.D. Add. 1566–79*, p. 428.

[4] *C.P.R. 1553–4*, p. 61.   [5] *A.P.C. 1554–6*, p. 210.

[6] Ibid., pp. 233, 300, 331–2.   [7] *C.S.P.D. Add. 1566–79*, p. 428.

[8] *A.P.C. 1575–7*, p. 43.

[9] Ibid. *1552–4*, pp. 218–19 ; Burgon, i. 106, 183, 466.

[10] Lans. MSS. 98, no. 11 ; Ascham, *Works*, ed. A. J. Giles, ii. 104–6, 122–3.

[11] Exch. K.R. Customs Accounts, 86/2, 6, 87/4, 167/1.

[12] Strype, ii. Appendix, p. 112.

payable within a year of his death, if his debts could be received out of Spain by that time.[1] In 1555 Fallowfield's wife had been 'enticed from her husbonde' by Francis Baringden, esquire, who was 'thought to lourke' with her in Kent, Bucks, Berks, or Oxon. For this enticement Baringden appeared before the Privy Council and was put under bond of 50 marks that he would 'from hensfourth refrayne the companye of the wief of Henry Fallowefelde'.[2] If this wife was Mary she must have been forgiven when Fallowfield made his will.

Henry Fisher. He may have been the merchant of the staple of that name who was a benefactor of the Skinners Company.[3]

Henry Flammacke. Flammacke was a grocer who was exporting cloth and importing mace and madder in the fifteen-fifties.[4] He died in January 1561, apparently without issue. His bequests included £50 to Christ's Hospital, 100 marks to his wife Alice, and £50 to his servant and brother-in-law, Richard Hancox.[5]

Nicholas Foljambe. No Nicholas appears among the Tudor Foljambes in Nathaniel Johnston's account of the family.[6] Perhaps he was the Genevan exile of that name in 1556, who may have been an illegitimate member of the Derbyshire Foljambes.[7] There was a Nicholas Foljambe, merchant of the staple, in 1558.[8]

Richard Foulkes. Foulkes was master of the Clothworkers in 1550 and an alderman from 1556 to 1560, when he secured his discharge on paying a fine of £200.[9] He was a merchant adventurer exporting cloth and wax and importing fustians.[10] Some at least of this trade was done with the Hanse towns.[11] He also imported silk from Antwerp and train oil, iron, and resin from Bayonne.[12] He was a charter assistant of the Russia Company and may have been its London agent in 1564.[13] Foulkes died about November 1570, leaving a mansion house, shop, and warehouses in London to his widow

---

[1] P.C.C. 17 Crymes.   [2] *A.P.C. 1554–6*, pp. 154, 163, 174.

[3] Lambert, p. 351.   [4] Exch. K.R. Customs Accounts, 86/6, 87/4.

[5] P.C.C. 5 Loftes.   [6] *Collectanea Topographica*, ii. 68–90.

[7] C. H. Garrett, *Marian exiles*, p. 155.

[8] *C.P.R. 1557–8*, p. 301.   [9] Beaven, i. 207, ii. 35.

[10] Patent Rolls, 8 Eliz., pt. 12 ; Exch. K.R. Customs Accounts, 86/6, 87/4, 90/11.

[11] Exch. K.R. Port Books, 2/1 ; *C.P.R. 1560–3*, p. 8.

[12] H.C.A. Examinations, 7 (10 March 1553), 17 (26 Sept. 1569).

[13] Exch. K.R. Customs Accounts, 90/11.

Elizabeth with reversion to his eldest son Austin,[1] who in 1588 was the chief agent of the Russia Company in Russia.[2]

Thomas Fraunces. He was presumably the merchant of that name who went out to Russia in the *Edward Bonaventure* in 1553.[3]

Sir John Gage, knight of the order, lord chamberlain of the household.[4]

Anthony Gamage. Gamage was the son of William Gamage and the grandson of John Gamage of Coity, Glamorgan.[5] He was a member of the Ironmongers Company, of which he was twice master, and an alderman from 1573 until his death in June 1579.[6] Gamage was a promoter of the Guinea voyage of 1558,[7] but he seems to have traded chiefly with France, to which he exported lead and wax and from which he imported canvas.[8] He also imported cottons [9] and was a charter member of the Spanish Company in 1577.[10] By 1569 he was an assistant of the Russia Company.[11] He was also a charter assistant of the Mineral and Battery Works [12] and a shareholder in the Mines Royal.[13] Apart from his interest in foreign trade, Gamage was a retailer of linen cloth,[14] and when he made his will in 1571 he had six apprentices, which suggests a considerable business. He left three houses in London worth £15 6s. 8d. p.a. and a personal estate worth more than £3600, from which he bequeathed £400 to the Ironmongers Company for loans.[15] His only son and heir William was master of the Ironmongers in 1603.[16]

William Garrard, alderman. Garrard was the son of John Garrard, citizen and grocer of London, and the grandson of William Garrard of Sittingbourne, Kent.[17] He was a haberdasher and master of the Haberdashers Company in 1557.[18] He was an alderman, 1547-71, mayor in 1555-6, when he was knighted, M.P. for London in 1557, and he died 27 September 1571.[19] Garrard was one of the great London merchants of his day. He was an

---

[1] P.C.C. 38 Lyon.
[2] Tolstoy, *Intercourse between England and Russia*, p. 295.
[3] Hakluyt, i. 245.   [4] *D.N.B.*, Sir John Gage, 1479-1556.
[5] Nicholl, p. 549.   [6] Beaven, ii. 39.   [7] H.C.A. Libels, 37. no. 247.
[8] Exch. K.R. Port Books, 4/2, 6/4.
[9] Exch. K.R. Customs Accounts, 90/11.
[10] Patent Rolls, 19 Eliz., pt. 8.   [11] Hakluyt, ii. 86.   [12] Carr, p. 19.
[13] Collingwood, *Elizabethan Keswick*, pp. 3-4.
[14] *C.S.P.D. 1547-80*, p. 620.
[15] P.C.C. 32 Bakon ; *Inq. p.m. Lond.*, iii. 21.   [16] Nicholl, p. 549.
[17] Strype, ii. bk. v. 133.   [18] Herbert, *Livery Companies*, ii. 539.
[19] Beaven, ii. 32.

assistant of the Merchant Adventurers' Company in 1564.[1] He exported cloth and molasses and imported camlets and dealt in silk.[2] He traded with Barbary, to which he exported cloth and from which he imported sugar.[3] He was among the promoters of the Guinea voyages of the 'fifties and 'sixties [4] and the slaving voyages of 1564 and 1567 [5] and was part owner of two ships engaged in the Guinea trade.[6] In addition to these activities, Garrard was a leading member of the Russia Company. He was one of the 'principall doers' of the first voyage of 1553 [7] and was a charter consul two years later. He was a governor of the company in 1561 [8] and 1567[9] and probably in 1569 [10] and 1570.[11] He was also a charter governor of the Mineral and Battery Works.[12]

Garrard seems to have prospered in his numerous enterprises. In the fifteen-forties he bought the manor of Southfleet, Kent, the manor of Dorney, Bucks, and land in Bermondsey, Surrey.[13] He was lending to the crown in 1560 and 1569.[14] This 'grave, sober, wise and discreet cittizen, equall with the best, and inferior to none',[15] left lands in Kent, Surrey, and Bucks to his wife and sons.[16] Of his children, Anne married George, son of Sir George Barne the elder,[17] William, the eldest son, inherited Dorney and Boveney in Bucks and was later knighted,[18] Peter may have been one of the Russia Company's servants in Persia in 1579,[19] and John was mayor in 1601-2 when he was knighted.[20]

Walter Garroway. Garroway was a draper, a merchant of the staple, and a merchant adventurer.[21] He died between 18 December 1571 and 28

---

[1] Patent Rolls, 6 Eliz., pt. 12.

[2] Exch. K.R. Customs Accounts, 86/6, 90/11 ; S.P.D. Eliz., vi. no. 52 ; xx. no. 63.　　[3] Exch. K.R. Port Books, 2/1, 3/2, 4/2.

[4] Williamson, *Sir John Hawkins*, pp. 40, 54 ; Hakluyt, iv. 133, 137.

[5] Williamson, op. cit., pp. 62, 129.　　[6] Ibid., p. 162 ; Blake, ii. 310.

[7] Stow, *Annales*, ed. 1631, p. 609.

[8] Hakluyt, ii. 4–9 ; Strype, *Sir Thomas Smith*, ed. 1820, p. 20 n.

[9] Hakluyt, ii. 50–1.　　[10] Ibid., ii. 86 ; Lans. MSS. 11, no. 37.

[11] Hakluyt, ii. 133 ; Tolstoy, *Intercourse between England and Russia*, p. 124.

[12] Carr, p. 19.

[13] Hasted, *Kent*, ed. 1797, ii. 429 ; *V.C.H. Bucks.*, iii. 223 ; *C.P.R. 1547–8*, p. 368.　　[14] *C.P.R. 1558–60*, pp. 353–4 ; Strype, i. bk. i. 283.

[15] Stow, i. 212.

[16] P.C.C. 3 Daper. He left a great standing cup of gilt to the Haberdashers from which 'ypocraze' was being drunk in 1583 (H. Ellis, *Original letters*, First Series, ii. 290).

[17] Hasted, p. 160.　　[18] P.C.C. 3 Daper ; *V.C.H. Bucks*, iii. 223.

[19] Hakluyt, ii. 171–201.　　[20] Beaven, ii. 44.

[21] Johnson, ii. 471, iii. 143 ; *C.P.R. 1558–60*, p. 24 ; *A.P.C. 1556–8*, p. 20.

February 1572, leaving a widow, four sons, and two daughters.[1] Three of his sons, Thomas, Francis, and Simon, later became free of the Drapers by patrimony.[2]

Edward Garth. He was probably the skinner and wool exporter who died in April or May 1555, apparently without issue.[3]

William Gifford. Gifford was probably a mercer, merchant adventurer, and merchant of the staple,[4] engaged in the export of wool to Calais and Hamburg and of cloth to Antwerp.[5] He seems to have imported friezadoes, buckram, pepper, wine, and flax.[6]

Edward Gilbert. Gilbert was probably the goldsmith who was an alderman from 1561 to 1564, when he secured his discharge on paying a fine of 100 marks, and who died in 1591.[7] In the 'fifties Gilbert was heavily engaged in buying and selling property, much of it formerly monastic.[8] He was an assistant of the Russia Company in 1569.[9]

Lawrence Glasier.

Thomas Goodman. He may have been the Thomas Goodman, mercer, who died in 1559 leaving lands in Essex and Surrey and a mansion in Leatherhead to his wife Margaret and their eleven children.[10]

Thomas Gravesend, gentleman. Gravesend was M.P. for Lewes in 1553 and 1555[11] and was appointed an assay master of the Mint in 1557.[12] In 1549 and 1553 he was buying property, much of it ex-chantry, in Sussex, Surrey, and London.[13]

Ralph Greneway. Greneway was born at Weston,[14] Norfolk, and became a member of the London Grocers Company of which he was master in 1557. He was an alderman from 1556 to 1558.[15] He exported cloth and imported

---

[1] P.C.C. 7 Daper. [2] Johnson, iii. 143.

[3] Exch. K.R. Customs Accounts, 87/7 ; P.C.C. 24 More.

[4] Patent Rolls, 6 Eliz., pt. 12 ; *C.P.R. 1558–60,* p. 24.

[5] Exch. K.R. Customs Accounts, 87/4, 7, 167/1 ; Exch. K.R. Port Books, 2/1, 5/6.

[6] Ibid. 4/2 ; Exch. K.R. Customs Accounts, 86/2, 6 ; Smit, ii. 987.

[7] Beaven, i. 4, ii. 36.

[8] *C.P.R. 1555–7,* p. 433 ; *1557–8,* pp. 336, 387–8.

[9] Hakluyt, ii. 86.   [10] P.C.C. 62 Chaynay.   [11] *Return,* i. 380, 394.

[12] *C.P.R. 1557–8,* p. 192.   [13] Ibid. *1549–51,* pp. 107–9 ; *1553,* p. 115.

[14] P.C.C. F 30 Noodes.   [15] Beaven, ii. 35.

wine, presumably from Spain, where his wife's brother, Richard Soday, acted as his servant or factor.[1]   He was a promoter of the Guinea voyage of 1558.[2]   Greneway died without issue in 1558 leaving a personal estate worth more than £4800, of which half went to his widow Katherine, who seems to have carried on as a wine importer,[3] and half to charities, servants, brothers and sisters, and nephews and nieces.[4]

Sir John Gresham the elder, knight and alderman.[5]   Sir John, the uncle of Thomas Gresham,[6] was a charter assistant of the Russia Company.

Thomas Gresham, esquire.[7]

Edward Griffin, esquire, attorney general.   Edward Griffin of Dingley, Northants, was the second son of Sir Nicholas Griffin of Braybrooke.[8] He was attorney general from 1552 to 1559.[9]   Griffin's will was proved on 14 July 1571.   He left a house and land to his third wife, Elizabeth, the widow of Sir Walter Stonor, lands in Northants, Derbyshire, and Leicestershire to his son Edward, £5000, with which land was to be bought, to his son Richard, and marriage portions of £500 and £300 to his daughters Anne and Margaret respectively.[10]

Henry Grover.   He was probably a draper and cloth exporter.[11]

Philip Gunter.   Gunter was born at Dyffryn, Monmouthshire,[12] and by 1537 was a member of the London Skinners Company,[13] of which he was later eight times master.   He was chosen an alderman in 1569, but secured his discharge on paying a fine of £400.[14]   Gunter carried on his business as skinner and upholsterer at his ' great house ', the Sarazen's Head in Cornhill, which he bought in 1553.[15]   He also seems to have sold ' upholsters wares ' in Oxford.[16]

---

[1] Exch. K.R. Customs Accounts, 86/6, 87/4 ; P.C.C. F 30 Noodes.

[2] H.C.A. Libels, 37. no. 247.

[3] *C.P.R. 1555–7*, p. 302.   She later married Sir John White (Beaven, ii. 172).

[4] P.C.C. F 30 Noodes.   [5] *D.N.B.*, Sir John Gresham, d. 1556.

[6] Burgon, i. 369–71 wrongly assumes that Sir John's nephew, Sir John Gresham the younger, was the charter member of the Russia Company.

[7] *D.N.B.*, Sir Thomas Gresham, 1519?–1579.

[8] *The visitations of Northamptonshire made in 1564 and 1618–19*, ed. W. C. Metcalfe, pp. 24, 120.

[9] E. Foss, *Tabulae curiales*, pp. 49–53.   [10] P.C.C. 32 Holney.

[11] Exch. K.R. Customs Accounts, 167/1 ; Boyd, p. 82.

[12] P.C.C. 8 Rowe.   [13] Herbert, *Livery companies*, ii. 302.

[14] Beaven, i. 182, ii. 38.   [15] Stow, i. 199, ii. 307.

[16] W. H. Turner, *Selections from the records of the city of Oxford*, pp. 218, 220.

There is little evidence that Gunter was actively engaged in foreign trade, but he supplied ' red lether skynnes for to lyne the gorgettes ' to the Drapers Company,[1] tapestry and bedding to Sir Henry Sidney,[2] and buckram for the court revels.[3] He died 15 February 1583 leaving three houses in London and land in Herts to his wife [4] and to his three sons and a considerable personal estate from which he made bequests to the poor of Monmouthshire and for repairing roads in that county.[5]

John Hare. He was probably John Hare, mercer, who was born at Homersfield, Suffolk, and who ' by his industry in his calling, left manours and lands, and tenements among his children '.[6] In the 'forties and 'fifties he was buying manors in Norfolk and Suffolk in company with his brother, Sir Nicholas Hare, Master of the Rolls.[7] His two daughters, Isabel and Margaret, had marriage portions of £300 each. Hare died in 1564 leaving property worth £200 p.a.[8]

John Harrison, goldsmith. Harrison was chosen alderman in 1574, but secured his discharge on payment of a fine of £200.[9] He was an assistant of the Russia Company in 1569 [10] and died about 1582.[11]

John Harshe. Perhaps he was the John Hasse, who was a merchant on the *Edward Bonaventure* in the voyage to Russia of 1553 and who wrote an account of Russian coinage, weights, and measures.[12]

Edmund Hasilfote.

William Hawtrey, gentleman. Hawtrey was a country gentleman of Chequers, Bucks,[13] and M.P. for Bucks in 1563.[14]

John Heathe. He was probably 'John Heathe, alias Heth, late of London, esq., late keeper of the Fleet prison, alias of London, esq., alias

---

[1] Johnson, ii. 412.

[2] *H.M.C. Lord de L'Isle and Dudley*, i. 259.

[3] Feuillerat, *Documents relating to the office of the revels in the time of Queen Elizabeth*, pp. 138, 158, 174, 184.

[4] Anne, daughter of Henry Barley of Albury, Herts (Strype, i. bk. ii. 146).

[5] P.C.C. 8 Rowe ; *Inq. p.m. Lond.*, iii. 58–60.

[6] Strype, i. bk. iii. 36, 38.

[7] *Letters and Papers, Henry VIII*, xxi. pt. i. 682–3 ; *C.P.R. 1555–7*, pp. 97–8.

[8] P.C.C. 5 Morrison.   [9] Beaven, i. 63, ii. 230.

[10] Hakluyt, ii. 86.   [11] Beaven, ii. 230.

[12] Hakluyt, i. 245, 294–9.   [13] *V.C.H. Bucks.*, ii. 336–7, iii. 25.

[14] *Return*, i. 403.

merchant of London and free of the company of the cowpers of the said citie '.[1] He seems to have been an importer and a retailer of wines.[2]

Thomas Heigham. He was probably an army officer who died at Calais in 1558, apparently without issue.[3]

Henry Herdson, alderman. Herdson was a member of the Skinners Company in 1537 [4] and its master in 1552. He was an alderman from 1554 until his death on 17 December 1555.[5] In the 'forties and 'fifties he was dealing extensively in monastic and chantry lands.[6] Herdson, who was a charter assistant of the Russia Company, was a cloth exporter [7] and a trader in Spanish oranges, oil, and wine.[8] He left lands in Kent, of which one-third went to his eldest son, Thomas, and two-thirds to his four younger sons. He seems also to have owned property in Somerset.[9]

George and Thomas Heton.[10] It is impossible to be certain of the Hetons' identity. George, who was a charter assistant of the Russia Company, was probably the merchant tailor, merchant of the staple, and cloth exporter,[11] who received an annuity of 20 marks from the Merchant Tailors in 1563 because of his losses by land and sea.[12] He seems to have had a brother Thomas,[13] who may have been the member of the Russia Company, and who seems to have been a mercer and cloth exporter.[14]

Rowland Heyward. Heyward, the son of George Heyward of Bridgnorth, Shropshire, went up to London as a boy and was apprenticed to a clothworker.[15] He was master of the Clothworkers Company in 1559, an

---

[1] *C.P.R. 1558–60*, p. 237.   [2] *A.P.C. 1558–70*, p. 13 ; *C.P.R. 1554–5*, p. 235.

[3] *C.S.P. For. 1553–8*, pp. 352–3 ; P.C.C. F 13 Noodes.

[4] Herbert, *Livery companies*, ii. 302.

[5] Beaven, ii. 34 ; *C.P.R. 1560–3*, pp. 372–3.

[6] *Letters and Papers, Henry VIII*, xxi. pt. i. 693, 767, ii. 100, 244 ; *C.P.R. 1549–51*, pp. 374–86.   [7] Exch. K.R. Customs Accounts, 87/4.

[8] Marsden, i. 112–13 ; Smit, i. 573.

[9] P.C.C. 38 More. For the fanciful attempt to prove that Herdson was an ancestor of Henry Hudson, the navigator, see J. M. Read, *A historical inquiry concerning Henry Hudson*, ed. E. Goldsmid, Clarendon Society's Historical Reprints, Series I (1882–4).

[10] The name is also spelt Eton.

[11] *C.P.R. 1553–4*, p. 425 ; Exch. K.R. Customs Accounts, 87/4, 167/1.

[12] Clode, i. 192 ; Clode, *Memorials*, pp. 534–5.

[13] *C.P.R. 1550–3*, pp. 74–5.   [14] Exch. K.R. Port Books, 2/1.

[15] W. Jay, ' Sir Rowland Hayward ', *Trans. London and Middlesex Archaeological Society*, N.S., vi. 509–27.

alderman from 1560 to 1593, mayor in 1570-1, when he was knighted, and again in 1591, and M.P. for London, 1572-81. He died on 5 December 1593.[1] Heyward was a merchant adventurer,[2] an exporter of cloth, an importer of fustians, camlets, and buckram,[3] and a dealer in silk.[4] He was a promoter of the third slaving voyage of 1567 [5] and a governor of the Mineral and Battery Works in 1568.[6] In addition to these activities, Heyward was an active member of the Russia Company, being a charter assistant in 1555 and a governor in 1567,[7] 1574,[8] 1577,[9] 1580,[10] and 1587.[11]

Heyward obviously prospered as a merchant. In 1553 he was buying extensive property, some of it formerly monastic, in four counties,[12] and ten years later he bought Elsing Spittal, which became his London house.[13] He was lending to the crown in 1560 and 1569.[14] His purchase of the manor of King's-hold, Hackney, in 1583 provided him with a country house, King's Place, where Elizabeth visited him in 1587.[15] He died a great landowner with property in London and more than a dozen manors in half a dozen counties. Most of this property went to the children of his second wife Catherine, the daughter of Thomas Smith and granddaughter of Sir Andrew Judde.[16]

Anthony Hickman. Hickman was a mercer,[17] a shipowner,[18] a cloth exporter, and a sugar importer.[19] His chief trade seems to have been with the Canaries, where he apparently traded in partnership with Edward Castelin.[20] He was also a promoter of the Guinea voyages of the fifteen-fifties and fifteen-sixties.[21]

John Hopkins. Hopkins, a charter assistant of the Russia Company, was probably the fishmonger and shipowner [22] who supplied fish for the navy

---

[1] Beaven, ii. 36. In 1560 he was said to have lived twenty-six years in London, which suggests that he was born about 1520 (H.C.A. Examinations, 13 (18 Oct. 1560)).   [2] Patent Rolls, 6 Eliz., pt. 12.

[3] Exch. K.R. Customs Accounts, 86/2, 6, 87/4 ; S.P.D. Eliz., vi. no. 52.

[4] Ibid., xx. no. 63.   [5] Williamson, *Sir John Hawkins*, p. 129.

[6] Carr, p. 19.   [7] Morgan and Coote, ii. 225.

[8] Collinson, *The three voyages of Martin Frobisher*, p. 89.

[9] Carr, p. 28.   [10] Hakluyt, ii. 203.   [11] Ibid., ii. 279.

[12] C.P.R. *1553-4*, pp. 478-9.   [13] Strype, i. bk. i. 154-5.

[14] C.P.R. *1558-60*, p. 353 ; Strype, i. bk. i. 283.   [15] Jay, op. cit., p. 518.

[16] P.C.C. 24 Darcy ; Inq. *p.m. Lond.*, iii. 202-210 ; Strype, i. bk. iii. 73-4.

[17] Herbert, *Livery companies*, i. 296.

[18] Hakluyt, i. 380-1 ; Oppenheim, *Administration of the royal navy*, pp. 122-3.

[19] Exch. K.R. Customs Accounts, 86/6, 87/4.   [20] Hakluyt, vi. 248.

[21] Ibid., iv. 47, 133, 137 ; Williamson, *Sir John Hawkins*, p. 54.

[22] H.C.A. Examinations, 10 (3 and 27 Nov. 1555) ; A.P.C. *1542-7*, pp. 347, 376, 410 ; *1556-8*, pp. 186-7.

in the fifteen-forties [1] and who traded with Antwerp, Spain, and Barbary.[2] He died between 27 December 1558 and 4 April 1559, leaving property in Surrey and London to his wife Joan and his son Richard,[3] who seems to have traded with Spain and Barbary.[4]

George Hopton. He was probably the George Hopton who gained his freedom of the Drapers Company by apprenticeship in 1545 [5] and who was importing wine, raisins, and figs in 1553–4,[6] presumably from Spain with which he was later trading.[7] In 1568 George Holmes was factor in Spain for Hopton and Thomas Moore, who may have been the charter member of that name.[8]

William, lord Howard of Effingham, lord high admiral.[9]

William Humfrey. Humfrey was a goldsmith and an assay master of the Mint.[10] With Christopher Shutz he received a patent in September 1565 for searching for minerals, including calamine, which he discovered in 1566. These activities led to the establishment of the Mineral and Battery Works in 1568, of which Humfrey was a charter assistant.[11] He was also a shareholder in the Mines Royal [12] and the inventor of improved methods of smelting lead.[13]

Anthony Hussey, esquire. Hussey, whom Machyn described as ' sqwyre, and a grett marchand-ventorer and of Muskovea and haburdassher ', was chief registrar to the Archbishop of Canterbury, a judge of the Court of Admiralty, a master in Chancery, and M.P. for Horsham in 1553 and for Shoreham in 1558.[14] He was a shipowner [15] and was governor of the Merchant Adventurers' Company from 1555 until at least 1559.[16] Hussey was a charter consul of the Russia Company and on Cabot's death he probably succeeded to the governorship of the company, though the only evidence for this is Hussey's epitaph which describes his as ' vergente demum aetate ad Praefectum

---

[1] *A.P.C. 1542–7*, p. 296.   [2] Blake, ii. 347–52.
[3] P.C.C. 3 Chaynay.   [4] Exch. K.R. Port Books, 2/1, 4/2.
[5] Boyd, p. 98.   [6] Exch. K.R. Customs Accounts, 86/2.
[7] Marsden, ii. 51.   [8] H.C.A. Examinations, 16 (28 Jan. 1568).
[9] *D.N.B.*, Lord William Howard, first baron Howard of Effingham, 1510?–1573.   [10] Strype, i. bk. i. 99.
[11] Carr, pp. xcvii–xcviii, 16, 19 ; W. R. Scott, *Joint-Stock Companies*, ii. 413–16.   [12] Collingwood, *Elizabethan Keswick*, pp. 3–4.
[13] J. W. Gough, *Mines of Mendip*, pp. 144–50.
[14] Machyn, pp. 236–7, 380 n. ; *Return*, i. 383, 398.
[15] *A.P.C. 1542–7*, pp. 374, 376, 410 ; Marsden, ii. 80–1.
[16] Johnson, ii. 118 n. ; *C.P.R. 1557–8*, p. 72 ; *1558–60*, p. 220.

Collegiorum Mercatorum Angliae, tam apud Belgas, quam apud Moscovitas, et Rhutenos commercia exercentium accitus '.[1] Hussey died 1 June 1560,[2] leaving property in London and his ' adventure in Russhaw ' to his wife Katherine and his son Lawrence.[3] Six years later the Russia Company bought Katherine's stock for £128.[4] Lawrence remained a member of the company, of which he was an assistant in 1569.[5]

Edward Jackman. Jackman was a grocer, and an alderman from 1561 until his death in September 1569. He married Anne, daughter of Humphrey Packington, who after his death married James Bacon, younger brother of Sir Nicholas and uncle of Francis Bacon.[6] Jackman was a merchant adventurer [7] and in 1569 an assistant of the Russia Company.[8] As a merchant Jackman traded in many commodities. His chief export seems to have been cloth to Antwerp and Barbary, but he also exported lead and saffron. He imported hops and rape oil from Antwerp, raisins from Malaga, and sugar from Barbary.[9] He was a promoter of the Guinea voyage of 1558.[10] In the 'fifties and 'sixties Jackman was buying and selling property in Norfolk, Northants, Yorks, Kent, and Sussex, often in company with his brother-in-law Richard Lambert.[11] At his death he owned property in Kent and Essex and a personal estate worth at least £8000, from which he bequeathed £200 to the Grocers Company for loans and £100 for London's water supply.[12]

Sir Henry Jerningham, knight and vice-chamberlain.[13]

Sir Andrew Judde, knight and alderman. Judde was the son of John Judde of Tonbridge and Margaret, daughter of Valentine Chiche and great-niece of archbishop Chichele. He was born about 1495 and was

---

[1] Strype, i. bk. iii. 176.   [2] Machyn, p. 236.
[3] P.C.C. 52 Mellershe. He also left £20 and his joint patent of the registrarship of St. Paul's to John Incent, willing him to bind up the register of archbishop Cranmer and the books of the archbishop and dean and chapter of Canterbury.
[4] Johnson, ii. 186, 454.   [5] Hakluyt, ii. 86.
[6] Beaven, ii. 37, 172.   [7] Patent Rolls, 6 Eliz., pt. 12.
[8] Hakluyt, ii. 86.
[9] Exch. K.R. Port Books, 2/1, 4/2 ; Exch. K.R. Customs Accounts, 86/2, 6, 87/4, 90/11.   [10] H.C.A. Libels, 37. no. 247.
[11] *C.P.R. 1554-5*, pp. 230, 247 ; *1560-3*, p. 581 ; Hasted, *Kent*, ed. 1797, viii. 295 ; L. F. Salzman, *Calendar of post mortem inquisitions relating to Sussex*, Sussex Record Society, iii. 83-4. Jackman's will shows that Lambert was his brother-in-law.   [12] P.C.C. 3 Lyon.
[13] *D.N.B.*, Sir Henry Jerningham, d. 1571. Jerningham cannot have died in 1571, for his will is dated 15 August 1572 (P.C.C. 18 Peter). It was proved 27 May 1573.

apprenticed to John Buknell, a London skinner and merchant of the staple.[1] Judde became a member of the Skinners Company and was six times its master. He was an alderman, 1541–58, and mayor in 1550–1, when he was knighted ; he died 4 Sept. 1558.[2] He was a shipowner,[3] and an exporter of cloth and wool.[4] As a wool exporter to Calais he was a member of the Staplers' Company and was mayor of the staple in 1552, 1555, and 1558.[5] Judde was a charter assistant of the Russia Company and a consul of the company in 1556.[6] According to his epitaph :

> To Russia and Muscova,
> To Spayne Gynny withoute fable,
> Traveld he, by land and sea,
> Bothe Mayre of London and Staple.[7]

There seems no evidence that Judde went to Russia, Spain, or Guinea,[8] but he was a promoter of the Guinea voyage of 1558.[9]

Judde became a rich man, partly perhaps through trade and partly through his third marriage in 1551 to the widow of Thomas Langton, a skinner, ' which was a rich mariadge, the inventorie amounting to sixe thousand poundes and more '.[10] Some of his wealth was used in founding six almshouses at St. Helen, Bishopsgate, and a free school at Tonbridge, which he endowed with property worth £60 3s. 8d. p.a.[11] He left lands in Kent, Surrey, and Herts, worth £141 p.a. to his third wife, Mary,[12] with reversion to John and Richard, the sons of his first marriage.[13] Alice, his only daughter by his first marriage, became the wife of Thomas Smith, the customer, and died in 1593 leaving money for the additional endowment of Judde's almshouses.[14]

John Kempe, the elder. Kempe, who was probably a draper,[15] died

---

[1] Lambert, pp. 176–7 ; R. Wilkinson, *Londina Illustrata*, i (no pagination).
[2] Beaven, ii. 30. [3] Hakluyt, i. 380–1.
[4] Exch. K.R. Customs Accounts, 87/4, 7, 167/1.
[5] *A.P.C.* 1552–4, p. 40 ; Clode, ii. 116 ; *C.P.R.* 1557–8, p. 300.
[6] J. Robertson, ' The first Russian embassy to England ', *Archaeological Journal*, xiii. 77–8. [7] Wilkinson, op. cit., i.
[8] The Bidding Prayer at Tonbridge School, which commemorates the founder, describes Judde as having gone to Russia and having crossed that country to Astrakhan, and also as having gone to the west coast of Africa. The Prayer is apparently a nineteenth-century fabrication (D. C. Somervell, *History of Tonbridge School*, pp. 11–12). [9] H.C.A. Libels, 37. no. 247.
[10] Wriothesley, *Chronicle*, ii. 46. [11] Stow, i. 113.
[12] P.C.C. 54 Welles ; and 58 Noodes.
[13] H. S. Vere Hodge, *Sir Andrew Judde*, p. 48.
[14] Lambert, pp. 351–2 ; Stow, i. 174.
[15] There were several drapers of that name (Boyd, p. 107 ; Johnson, ii. 396–7, 439–40).

sometime before 1569 leaving his stock in the Russia Company to his son John, who was a minor and who was to inherit the stock at the age of 24. During John's minority, the stock was administered by his uncle, another John Kempe, draper, who died between September and November 1569, leaving a personal estate worth at least £1000.[1]

Philip Kever. He was presumably the citizen and merchant of London of that name who was resident at Cadiz, where he died sometime between April and August 1555.[2] He may have been related to the Edward Kever who was a merchant on the *Bona Confidentia* in the voyage to Russia in 1553 and who probably perished when the ship was frozen in the ice.[3]

William Knight. On 23 March 1522 Knight was granted the succession to Sir William Thomas as ' troner and peiser ' of wool in London, but after Thomas's death in 1543, Knight seems to have surrendered the tronage and peisage of wool in exchange for the offices of master of gold and silver assays at the Mint and of vice-treasurer of the Tower.[4] He appears to have remained an assay master of the Mint until his death, which took place sometime before 21 July 1557.[5] If Knight is the Mint official of that name referred to in *A discourse of the common weal*, it is difficult to see how the *Discourse* could have been written in 1549, as Miss Lamond claimed, for he is there referred to as being dead [6] and he seems to have been alive in 1555.[7]

Francis Lambert. Lambert was a grocer,[8] a cloth exporter,[9] and a promoter of the Barbary voyage of 1552 and of the Guinea voyage of 1553.[10] He also traded with Spain.[11]

Thomas Langley. A merchant of this name was one of the twelve councillors appointed for the Russia voyage of 1553, but he is given as sailing

---

[1] P.C.C. 23 Sheffeld.   His bequests included £200 to Oxford and Cambridge, £100 to Sir William Cordell, and £100 to the parish church of St. George, Southwark, for interest-free loans to 20 poor occupiers.

[2] P.C.C. 31 More.   [3] Hakluyt, i. 246.

[4] A. F. Pollard, ' A protean clerk of the Commons ', *Bulletin of the Institute of Historical Research*, xviii. 49–50.   [5] *C.P.R. 1557–8*, p. 192.

[6] *A discourse of the common weal of this realm of England*, ed. E. Lamond, pp. 117–18, 191. Miss Lamond pointed out that Knight's name seemed to be a later insertion in the text, but even so the reference to Knight is difficult to explain.   [7] Ruding, *Annals of the coinage*, iii. 10.

[8] *C.P.R. 1553–4*, p. 427.

[9] Exch. K.R. Customs Accounts, 87/4, 167/1.

[10] Hakluyt, iv. 33 ; Williamson, *Sir John Hawkins*, p. 40.

[11] H.C.A. Examinations, 16 (3 June 1567).

in the *Bona Confidentia* [1] and all on board that ship perished when it was frozen in the ice. Perhaps he changed ship, or perhaps the charter member was a relative of the same name.

Walter Leveson. It does not seem possible to identify him unless he was the Walter Leveson who was a son of John Leveson, merchant of the staple and sheriff of Staffordshire in 1561-2. Walter died in 1562. [2]

William Leveson. He was a merchant of the staple and probably a mercer. [3]

John Lewes, notary public. Lewes seems to have been a merchant as well as a notary public and a proctor of the Arches. [4] He was in Scotland in February 1557 trying to recover the goods of the *Edward Bonaventure*, wrecked on the Scottish coast on its return from Russia, [5] and was imprisoned for having ' at his sadle crutche a dagger '. He was released by order of the council in Edinburgh. [6] He was still alive in 1580. [7]

William Lewkner. Lewkner was a draper and a cloth exporter. [8] He died in November or December 1558 leaving his stock of £111 in the Russia Company to his two sons, John and William, to whom he also left £33 6s. 8d. each. If both sons died before the age of 21, the stock was to go to his two unmarried daughters, Mary and Elizabeth, who were also left £40 each. Lewkner left £200 to his wife Joan, the daughter of John Broke, draper. [9]

Thomas Locke. Locke was the son of Sir William Locke [10] who died in 1550 leaving extensive property in London and lands in Surrey to his five sons. The London property included a number of shops which Sir William left to his sons ' to the intent that they may dwell in them and keep the retailing shop still in my name to continue there '. [11] Thomas seems to have added to his inheritance by buying former monastic and chantry property in Surrey

---

[1] Hakluyt, i. 241, 246.

[2] S. Shaw, *History and antiquities of Staffordshire*, ii. 169.

[3] *C.P.R. 1557-8*, p. 301 ; Burgon, ii. 502.

[4] Exch. K.R. Customs Accounts, 87/4 ; *C.P.R. 1558-60*, p. 201.

[5] J. Robertson, 'The first Russian embassy to England', *Archaeological Journal*, xiii. 77-8.

[6] E. Lodge, *Illustrations of British history*, i. 221, 224-5.

[7] *C.S.P.D. 1591-4*, pp. 281-2.

[8] Exch. K.R. Customs Accounts, 87/4 ; Boyd, p. 115.

[9] P.C.C. 21 Welles.

[10] For his pedigree see ' Historical account of the Locke family ', *Gentleman's Magazine*, 1792, ii. 798-801.   [11] *Inq. p.m. Lond.*, i. 80-3.

in 1553.[1] He was a mercer, a cloth exporter,[2] and one of the promoters of the Guinea voyage of 1554.[3] He seems to have traded with Antwerp [4] and to have acted as one of Henry VIII's agents there.[5] He died 26 October 1556 [6] leaving property worth £55 p.a. to his wife Mary, apparently a sister of Anthony Hickman, and to his four sons, of whom the eldest, William, died on 28 October 1558.[7] Locke's brother, Michael, was London agent of the Russia Company in 1575.[8]

Thomas Lodge, alderman.[9] It is possible to supplement the *D.N.B.* account of Lodge's business activities. In 1548 Lodge was engaged in marine insurance as an underwriter of the *Santa Maria* of Venice on a voyage from Cadiz to London.[10] Ten years later he was trading with France.[11] Lodge was a merchant of the staple exporting wool to Calais in 1554-5.[12] In 1559 he received a licence to export 70 sarplers of wool to foreign parts beyond ' lez streightes ' of Morocco.[13] He was also a merchant adventurer, exporting cloth in 1547, 1553-4, and 1559,[14] and importing sugar in 1553-4 and linen, ginger, and pepper in 1556-7.[15] He was one of the merchants ' trading and occupying ' silk in 1561.[16] Lodge was trading with Barbary in 1555 [17] and was a promoter of the Guinea voyages of 1558, 1561, 1563, and 1564 as well as of the slaving voyage of 1562.[18] The *D.N.B.* appears to assume incorrectly that all these voyages to the Guinea coast were connected with the slave trade. Lodge was a charter assistant of the Russia Company and a governor in 1561 [19] and perhaps also in 1566.[20] It is difficult to reconcile some of this trading activity with Stow's story that Lodge went bankrupt in 1563.[21] Lodge's dispute during his mayoralty of 1562-3 with Edward Skeggs, the purveyor, can hardly have

[1] *C.P.R. 1553*, pp. 194-5.

[2] Exch. K.R. Customs Accounts, 87/4, 167/1.   [3] Hakluyt, iv. 47.

[4] H. Ellis, *Original letters*, Second Series, ii. 175.

[5] *C.P.R. 1547-8*, p. 233.   [6] Ibid. *1555-7*, pp. 455-6.

[7] P.C.C. 26 Ketchyn ; *Inq. p.m. Lond.*, i. 225-8.

[8] Hakluyt, ii. 158. Michael's surname is often spelt Lok.

[9] *D.N.B.*, Sir Thomas Lodge, d. 1584. For a more accurate account of Lodge's family than that given in the *D.N.B.*, see C. J. Sisson, ed. *Thomas Lodge and other Elizabethans*.

[10] Marsden, ii. 47-8.   [11] *A.P.C. 1556-8*, pp. 268-9.

[12] *C.P.R. 1553-4*, p. 446 ; Exch. K.R. Customs Accounts, 87/7.

[13] *C.P.R. 1558-60*, pp. 93-4.

[14] Exch. K.R. Customs Accounts, 87/4, 167/1 ; S.P.D. Eliz., vi. no. 52 ; Smit, i. 757.   [15] Exch. K.R. Customs Accounts, 86/2, 6.

[16] S.P.D. Eliz., xx. no. 63.   [17] Blake, ii. 347-8.

[18] H.C.A. Libels, 37. no. 247 ; Hakluyt, iv. 133, 137 ; vii. 5 ; Williamson, *Sir John Hawkins*, p. 54.   [19] Hakluyt, ii. 4-9.   [20] Ibid., ii. 35-40.

[21] J. Gairdner, *Three fifteenth-century chronicles*, pp. 126-8.

ruined him. Hall suggests that at this time Lodge was called upon to meet heavy financial obligations to his former apprentice, George Stoddard, but the account of Lodge's dealings with Stoddard is so obscure that little can be concluded from it.[1] It is clear that Lodge was in severe financial difficulties in 1567, for he was then a prisoner in the Fleet for a debt of £2500. To secure his release the Drapers Company lent him £200, but on the security of two members of his own company, the Grocers.[2] How Lodge finally extricated himself from his financial difficulties is not known, but when he died in 1584 he left property in Staffordshire and some personal estate, including a good deal of plate. The bequest of £10 and of the remission of the remaining years of service of his apprentice, Luke Williams, suggests that Lodge was still in business when he made his will in 1583. Lodge left nothing, not even a piece of plate, to his second son, Thomas, the poet and dramatist, who was not mentioned in the will, though his brothers were.[3]

Edmund Lomnour, esquire, and **Katherine Lomnour,** late wife of Richard Wigmour deceased. The Wigmours or Wigmores seem to have been a Herefordshire family related to the Hakluyts.[4] Richard was presumably a subscriber to the Russia voyage of 1553, which would account for his late wife's presence as a charter member in 1555. He died sometime before 14 July 1553, leaving his great house in Mark Lane and two tenements to Katherine for life and lands in Kent and Hampshire to his sons, Thomas and William.[5] Edmund Lomnour held the surveyorship of petty customs and subsidy in the port of London under a grant of 21 September 1531,[6] but he seems to have surrendered this office in 1549.[7] At his death in 1558 he was described as of Mannington, Norfolk. He left 2200 acres in Norfolk to his wife Katherine for life with reversion to his son Edmund. Katherine was to have full discretion in the use of the portions which Richard Wigmour had left to his children.[8]

Evan Lucie. He was the son of Humphrey Lucie, leatherseller, who died 17 August 1549 and from whom he inherited the manor of Bromley Hall, Middlesex.[9]

---

[1] Hall, *Society in the Elizabethan age*, pp. 50–1.

[2] Johnson, ii. 160–1.

[3] P.C.C. 29 Brudenell. Thomas, the son, had inherited property from his mother who died in 1579 (E. W. Gosse, *Memoir of Thomas Lodge*, 1883, p. 5).

[4] E. G. R. Taylor, *The original writings and correspondence of the two Richard Hakluyts*, i. 3.   [5] P.C.C. F 15 Tashe.

[6] *Letters and Papers, Henry VIII*, xxi. pt. i. 680.

[7] *C.P.R. 1549–51*, p. 65.   [8] P.C.C. F 50 Noodes.

[9] *Inq. p.m. Lond.*, i. 106–7 ; *C.P.R. 1549–51*, p. 236.

Richard Mallory. Mallory, the son of Anthony Mallory of Papworth, Cambridgeshire,[1] was a mercer and was three times master of the Mercers Company. He was an alderman, 1556–67, mayor in 1564–5, when he was knighted, and he died in March 1567.[2] Mallory was a merchant adventurer,[3] an exporter of cloth, and an importer of sugar and sarcenet.[4] In 1549 he paid £128 for former chantry property in West Cheap consisting of a house with courts, chambers, shops, cellars, solars, stables, and gardens, which he already occupied as tenant.[5] He seems also to have maintained a country house at Walgrave, Northants, and to have owned farms in Northants and Leicestershire.[6] Mallory had a very large family by his first wife, Anne, the daughter of Robert Packington, who died in 1560 in giving birth to her seventeenth child.[7] Of the daughters of this marriage, Anne had a portion of £200 on her marriage to Thomas Downes, and Scholastica 400 marks on her marriage to William Kelf. Mallory left his stock in the Russia Company to his six sons, one of whom, Richard, was to be apprenticed to an honest merchant. He also left £60 to each of his four unmarried daughters in addition to their share of the children's third.[8]

William Mallory. William's ownership of the manor of Papworth St. Agnes [9] suggests that he was related to Richard Mallory. He seems to have been M.P. for Hunts in 1555 [10] and to have been knighted sometime before 18 January 1558.[11] He was a charter assistant of the Russia Company, a mercer, and a cloth exporter.[12]

Christopher Marler. He may have been a member of the Kentish family of that name,[13] and was probably the merchant tailor who died towards the end of 1576, apparently without issue. He left lands in Yorkshire to John and William Jenkinson, his sister's grandsons, and 40s., a stone pot covered with silver, a silver trencher salt with a cover, and his black wearing gown to his ' Nurce Sybell Broke '.[14]

Walter Marler.[15] He was a haberdasher, a merchant adventurer, and a cloth exporter.[16]

---

[1] Herbert, *Livery companies*, i. 248 n.

[2] Beaven, ii. 35.   [3] Patent Rolls, 6 Eliz., pt. 12.

[4] Exch. K.R. Customs Accounts, 86/2, 6, 87/4, 167/1 ; Exch. K.R. Port Books, 2/1.   [5] *C.P.R. 1548–9*, p. 238 ; Strype, i. bk. iii. 37.

[6] P.C.C. 9 Stonarde.   [7] Beaven, ii. 172 ; Machyn, pp. 232, 379.

[8] P.C.C. 9 Stonarde.   [9] *C.P.R. 1547–8*, p. 327.

[10] *Return*, i. 393.   [11] *C.P.R. 1557–8*, p. 65.

[12] Exch. K.R. Port Books, 6/4.   [13] Hasted, *Kent*, ed. 1797, ii. 280.

[14] P.C.C. 1 Daughtry.   [15] His name is also spelt Merler.

[16] *C.P.R. 1558–60*, p. 169 ; Exch. K.R. Customs Accounts, 87/4, 167/1 ; Burgon, i. 259.

John Marshe [1] the younger, esquire. Marshe came of a Northants family and was the owner of the manor of Sywell in that county.[2] He married Alice, daughter of William Gresham and cousin of Sir Thomas Gresham.[3] His daughter Judith married Anthony Jenkinson, who was employed by the Russia Company in opening up its trade with Persia.[4] Marshe seems to have been M.P. for Reading in 1547 and for London on six occasions between 1553 and 1572.[5] He died about 1578.[6] Marshe was a mercer, a merchant of the staple,[7] a cloth exporter,[8] and a shipowner.[9] He was a merchant adventurer and governor of the Merchant Adventurers' Company in 1555,[10] 1559,[11] 1564,[12] 1565,[13] 1569,[14] 1570,[15] and 1572.[16] He was one of the promoters of the Spanish Company and its charter president in 1577.[17]

Roger Martin. Martin was the son of Lawrence Martin of Long Melford, Suffolk.[18] He was a mercer and twice master of the Mercers Company, an alderman, 1556–73, and mayor in 1567–8, when he was knighted; he died 20 December 1573.[19] Martin was a merchant of the staple[20] and a merchant adventurer.[21] His chief business seems to have been the export of cloth.[22] In 1570 he was importing silk from Hamburg where he had two factors.[23] He was a rich man, buying property in Gloucestershire in 1553 and

---

[1] His name is often spelt Mershe.

[2] Morgan and Coote, i. lxxxix–xci ; *V.C.H. Northampton*, iv. 133.

[3] *Miscellanea genealogica et heraldica*, N.S., iv. 254.

[4] Morgan and Coote, passim.

[5] *Return*, i. 375, 379, 386, 397, 404, 409 ; Appendix. xxxiv.

[6] Burgon, ii. 64 n.   [7] *C.P.R. 1558–60*, p. 232.

[8] Exch. K.R. Customs Accounts, 87/4 ; S.P.D. Eliz., vi. no. 52.

[9] H.C.A. Examinations, 18 (7 Nov. 1570).

[10] Smit, i. 757.   [11] *C.S.P. For. 1558–9*, pp. 504, 574.

[12] Patent Rolls, 6 Eliz., pt. 12. Lingelbach, *The Merchant Adventurers of England*, p. 232, gives the charter governor's name as John Marth, but Lingelbach printed the charter, not from the Patent Rolls, but from the seventeenth-century copy in S.P.D. Charles II, xxvii, where the name is wrongly given as Marth. It is time for a new edition of Lingelbach's *Merchant Adventurers*.

[13] *C.S.P. For. 1564–5*, p. 456.   [14] Smit, ii. 1003.

[15] *A.P.C. 1558–70*, p. 357 ; H.C.A. Examinations, 18 (7 Nov. 1570).

[16] R. G. Usher, *Court of High Commission*, p. 354.

[17] Patent Rolls, 19 Eliz., pt. 8 ; *C.S.P.D. Add. 1566–79*, p. 505.

[18] Overall, p. 308 n.   [19] Beaven, ii. 35.

[20] *C.P.R. 1558–60*, p. 411.

[21] Patent Rolls, 6 Eliz., pt. 12 ; Burgon, i. 259, 466.

[22] Exch. K.R. Customs Accounts, 87/4, 167/1 ; Exch. K.R. Port Books, 2/1 ; S.P.D. Eliz., vi. no. 52.

[23] H.C.A. Examinations, 18 (25 and 29 Nov. 1570).

in Nottinghamshire in 1559 [1] and lending large sums to the crown. In 1558 he shared with three others in a loan of £18,000 to the crown [2] and lent £1500 in 1569.[3] He maintained a house in Soper Lane, London, and another at Hoxton, Middlesex.[4] Martin was twice married. His first wife was Letitia, daughter of Humphrey Packington, and his second, Elizabeth, daughter of William Castelin and widow of Thomas Knowles, a London mercer.[5] The children of these marriages were amply provided for. Two daughters, Susan and Martha, received marriage portions of 500 marks each, and a third daughter, Mary, received £1000 on her marriage to Alexander Denton. Two sons, Humphrey and Edmund, received £500 each during Martin's lifetime. At his death Martin disposed of his third of his personal estate in bequests which exceeded £3000. They included £200 to the Mercers for loans and £40 for a dinner, £100 to the London hospitals and £40 to London prisons, £50 each to Oxford and Cambridge Universities, £66 13s. 4d. to poor householders of Long Melford where he was born, and legacies to servants, apprentices, friends, and relations. His widow, in addition to her third of the personal estate, received a legacy of £333 6s. 8d., and the use of the London and Hoxton houses for life. The children, in addition to the sums they had received during their father's lifetime and in addition to their share of their third of the personal estate, received £200 each in the case of the two sons, Edmund and Humphrey, £250 each in the case of the unmarried daughters, Joan and Anne, 200 marks each in the case of the married daughters, Susan and Martha, and £200 in the case of Mary Denton.[6]

Alexander Mather.

John Medley. He seems to have been a merchant of the staple [7] and the holder of a patent for an engine for draining mines.[8]

William Merick. Merick was born about 1517 at Kingswood, Wilts, and came up to London at the age of 14.[9] He became a merchant tailor [10] and a cloth exporter engaged in trade with Spain.[11] He was a charter member of

[1] *C.P.R. 1553–4*, p. 363 ; *1558–60*, p. 377.
[2] Ibid. *1557–8*, p. 434.   [3] Burgon, ii. 342.
[4] P.C.C. 1 Martyn.   [5] Overall, 308 n.
[6] P.C.C. 1 Martyn. Susan married Robert Lie or Ley, and Martha married John Castelin. Martin left a standing cup to Bread Street Ward, where he was alderman, to be used at the time of the wardmote inquest.
[7] *C.P.R. 1557–8*, p. 300 ; Exch. K.R. Customs Accounts, 87/7.
[8] *C.P.R. 1560–3*, pp. 531–2 ; E. W. Hulme, ' History of the patent system ', *Law Quarterly Review*, xii. 146.
[9] H.C.A. Examinations, 13 (28 Feb. 1560).
[10] Clode, ii. 341.   [11] Exch. K.R. Port Books, 2/1.

the Spanish Company of 1577.[1]   He was also concerned in marine insurance [2] and was a promoter of the Guinea voyage of 1558.[3]   Merick was an employee as well as a member of the Russia Company.   He seems to have been the London agent of the company sometime before 1567 [4] and to have been appointed chief agent in Russia in 1573.[5]   In 1580 he agreed to serve the company for two years at a salary of £100 p.a. and a share of the profits which he estimated should amount to £150 p.a.   Merick did not fulfil this contract of service for he died sometime before 4 August 1581.[6]   His second son, John, was successively agent, member, and governor of the company. He was ambassador to Russia in the early seventeenth century and was knighted in 1614.[7]

James Mershe, gentleman.

George Milles.   He may have been the military engineer or contractor who was paid £800 in 1546 for building fortifications on the Isle of Wight,[8] and who was a commissioner for surveying the fortifications of Guernsey and Jersey in 1562.[9]

John Milner.   He was probably the John Miller or Milner, merchant tailor and merchant of Antwerp,[10] who was an importer of canvas and buckram and an exporter of cloth.[11]   He may also have been a charter assistant of the Merchant Adventurers' Company in 1564.[12]

Thomas Moore.   Moore cannot be identified with certainty, but he was probably a merchant of the staple [13] and a cloth exporter.[14]   A Thomas Moore was an assistant of the Russia Company in 1569.[15]

Miles Mording.   Mording, who was a charter assistant of the Russia

---

[1] Patent Rolls, 19 Eliz., pt. 8.

[2] Marsden, ii. 46 ; cf. *A.P.C. 1578–80*, p. 360.

[3] H.C.A. Libels, 37. no. 247.

[4] Morgan and Coote, ii. 211 ; Harl. MSS. 253, f. 16d.

[5] J. Hamel, *England and Russia*, p. 222 ; Tolstoy, *Intercourse between England and Russia*, p. 154.

[6] P.C.C. 29 Darcy.   [7] *D.N.B.*, Sir John Meyrick, d. 1638.

[8] *Letters and Papers, Henry VIII*, xxi. pt. i. 312.

[9] *C.P.R. 1560–3*, pp. 276–7, 425–6.   [10] Ibid. *1554–5*, p. 357.

[11] Exch. K.R. Customs Accounts, 86/2, 6 ; Exch. K.R. Port Books, 2/1.

[12] Patent Rolls, 6 Eliz., pt. 12.

[13] *C.P.R. 1557–8*, p. 301 ; Exch. K.R. Customs Accounts, 87/7.

[14] Ibid. 87/4, 167/1.

[15] Hakluyt, ii. 86.

Company, was an exporter of cloth, and an importer of tapestry.[1] In 1556 he was preparing goods in Flanders to ship to Bristol and from there to the Guinea coast, but as the Guinea trade was at that time forbidden, he was put under bond of £500 not to proceed with the voyage.[2] When the prohibition had been removed, he became a promoter of the Guinea voyage of 1558.[3] Mording died 19 November 1563. His will describes him as a skinner. He left four messuages in the parish of St. Nicholas, Cornhill, value £8 3s. 4d. p.a., which had formerly belonged to the college of Acon and which he had bought from Philip Bold in 1559, and lands in Staffordshire. This property went to his widow Alice for life with reversion to his son George, who was to pay £100 to Mording's daughters, Anne and Sarah, on their marriages. He also left £10 to his apprentice Richard Downes and £3 6s. 8d. to his servant, Erasmus.[4]

William Mounslowe. He seems to have been a mercer who was buying monastic property in London in 1538.[5]

Thomas Nicholes the elder, mercer. Nicholes was a cloth exporter [6] and a promoter of the Guinea voyage of 1558.[7] In 1555 he bought the manor of Mardleybury, Herts, from Nicholas Throckmorton, but sold it the following year to John Forster.[8] He died on 31 May 1561 leaving 5 messuages, 6 tenements, and 7 cottages in London, value £26 13s. 4d. p.a., part of which went to his son Anthony and part to his widow Elizabeth with reversion to Anthony. He also left property in Clerkenwell, Tottenham, and Islington to his eldest son Robert, aged 12, and £100 to each of his children, Mary, Elizabeth, Richard, Christiana, and Susan. Nicholes appointed his brother-in-law, Richard Springham, as sole executor and guardian of his three sons.[9]

Thomas Nicholes, goldsmith. He may have been the citizen and goldsmith of London who published in 1550 a translation of Thucydides from the French version of Claude de Seyssel.[10] A Thomas Nicholes, who may have been the same man, was secretary of the Russia Company in the fifteen-

---

[1] Exch. K.R. Customs Accounts, 86/2, 6, 87/4 ; S.P.D. Eliz., vi. no. 52.

[2] *A.P.C. 1554–6*, pp. 322, 347, 384.

[3] H.C.A. Libels, 37. no. 247.

[4] P.C.C. 36 Chayre ; *Inq. p.m. Lond.*, ii. 25–6.

[5] *Letters and Papers, Henry VIII*, xxi. pt. i. 717.

[6] Exch. K.R. Customs Accounts, 87/4, 167/1 ; S.P.D. Eliz., vi. no. 52.

[7] H.C.A. Libels, 37. no. 247.

[8] *C.P.R. 1554–5*, p. 13 ; *1555–7*, p. 6.

[9] P.C.C. 3 Streat ; *Inq. p.m. Lond.*, ii. 180–1.

[10] *D.N.B.*, Thomas Nichols, fl. 1550.

sixties[1] and perhaps also in 1556.[2] The Merchant Adventurers' Company seems also to have had a secretary of that name in 1555.[3]

Thomas Offley the elder, alderman.[4] There seems so little evidence of Offley's business activities that it is not possible to add much to the scanty account in the *D.N.B.* Offley was a charter assistant of the Russia Company, but he does not seem ever to have been a consul or a governor. The customs records suggest that his main business as a merchant was in the export of wool;[5] he does not figure among the cloth exporters, nor does he appear to have been a merchant adventurer.

James Paget, gentleman.

William, lord Paget of Beaudesert.[6]

Thomas Palley the elder. Palley, who was a charter assistant of the Russia Company, was a fishmonger and an importer of fish from the Low Countries.[7] He died towards the end of 1558, leaving property in Surrey, Essex, Wilts, Hants, and Berks to his eldest son John, as well as property at Croydon to his second son Thomas and two houses in London to his third son William. He also left £50 to the Fishmongers Company for loans, £5 to his journeyman, James Plogg, who was to help his, Palley's, widow in making a reckoning of debts, £5 to his 'lad' Jerome Warren, who was to be bound apprentice to some honest cook, and £2 to each of an unspecified number of apprentices, who were also to be released from one year's service.[8] Such remission of part of an apprentice's term of service was not uncommon in merchants' wills.

Anthony Pargetoure. Pargetoure was a merchant of the staple and a wool exporter.[9] In 1553 he was exporting herrings from Middelburg to France.[10]

---

[1] S.P.D. Eliz., xxxv. no. 23 ; Hakluyt, ii. 33–40.
[2] J. Robertson, 'The first Russian embassy to England', *Archaeological Journal*, xiii. 79.
[3] Smit, i. 757. Neither Thomas Nicholes, mercer, nor Thomas Nicholes, goldsmith, should be confused with the Thomas Nicholas, who acted as factor for Hickman and Castelin in the Canaries and whom the *D.N.B.* apparently makes into two people (Thomas Nicholas, fl. 1560–96, and Thomas Nichols, fl. 1554).   [4] *D.N.B.*, Sir Thomas Offley, 1505?–1582.
[5] Exch. K.R. Customs Accounts, 87/7 ; cf. *A.P.C. 1581–2*, pp. 83–4.
[6] *D.N.B.*, William Paget, first baron Paget of Beaudesert, 1505–63.
[7] Smit, i. 744, 747.   [8] P.C.C. 17 Welles.
[9] *C.P.R. 1557–8*, p. 301 ; Exch. K.R. Customs Accounts, 87/7.
[10] Smit, i. 749.

Richard Patrickes. Patrickes was a haberdasher whose chief trade was with Rouen, to which he exported cloth and from which he imported wool cards, playing-cards, combs, and possibly linen and canvas.[1] He also exported cottons and wax, and imported onions and probably herrings.[2] He seems to have been appointed controller of the custom and subsidy of tonnage and poundage in London in 1553,[3] and to have gone with Hugh Offley to Rouen in 1569 to secure the release of goods stayed by the French.[4] Patrickes was a man of some property, for he sold the manor of Woolwich for £2000 in 1578.[5]

William, earl of Pembroke.[6] The *D.N.B.* states that Pembroke was a promoter of a voyage to Africa in 1563. This presumably refers to the second slaving voyage of 1564, of which he was a promoter.[7]

Sir William Petre, knight, principal secretary.[8]

Richard Pointer. Pointer was apprenticed to a draper in 1517 and was later a warden of the Drapers Company.[9] He was an assistant of the Russia Company, a merchant adventurer, and a cloth exporter.[10] He imported linen and woad.[11] Pointer died early in 1564, leaving his house in Coleman Street to his wife, Joan, for life with reversion to his son Vincent, who seems to have been his only child. He left £6 13s. 4d. to his apprentice, William Harper, and the remission of a year's service, £100 to his kinswoman and servant, Beatrix Doix, £20 to London for repairing and amending water pipes, and £20 to the poor of St. Stephen, Coleman Street, to be distributed in charcoal at the rate of three loads p.a. Pointer's will suggests that he was a native of, or had some connexion with, Shrewsbury, to which he left £10 for bringing water and repairing bridges. He also had a house in Shrewsbury, in which his sister Elizabeth Skinner had lately dwelt, and which he left to Roger Haines, shearman, of Shrewsbury.[12]

---

[1] Exch. K.R. Port Books, 2/1, 4/2 ; *C.P.R. 1550–3*, pp. 95–6.

[2] Exch. K.R. Customs Accounts, 86/6, 90/11 ; H.C.A. Examinations, 8 (7 July 1553).

[3] *C.P.R. 1553*, p. 392. It is not quite certain that this was the same man, for the grant describes him as ' gentleman '.

[4] *C.S.P. For. 1569–71*, pp. 89, 100, 107.   [5] Hasted, pp. 149–50.

[6] *D.N.B.*, Sir William Herbert, first earl Pembroke of the second creation, 1501?–70.   [7] Williamson, *Sir John Hawkins*, p. 92.

[8] *D.N.B.*, Sir William Petre, 1505?–72.

[9] Boyd, p. 146 ; Johnson, ii. 470.

[10] *C.P.R. 1558–60*, p. 172 ; Exch. K.R. Customs Accounts, 87/4, 167/1.

[11] Exch. K.R. Customs Accounts, 86/6 ; H.C.A. Examinations, 10 (16 Oct. 1555).   [12] P.C.C. 9 Stevenson.

Edward Pryme, citizen and merchant of Bristol. Edward Pryme or Prynn was a founder of the Bristol Merchant Venturers' Company and its first master in 1552.[1]

John Quarles. Quarles was apprenticed to a draper in 1524 and was later twice master of the Drapers Company.[2] He was a merchant adventurer, exporting cloth to Antwerp,[3] and was an assistant of the Merchant Adventurers' Company in 1564.[4] He seems to have supplied the Russia Company with kerseys, which the company exported to Persia.[5] He was an assistant of the company in 1569.[6] Quarles died between October 1577 and January 1578, leaving a large personal estate from which his second wife, Agnes, received £3000 and his five sons and three daughters received £3075 in all in addition to £2770 which they had received during their father's lifetime. Quarles left £200 to the Drapers Company and £100 to the Merchant Adventurers' Company for loans, as well as numerous bequests to servants, hospitals, and the poor. His bequests to the poor of Blakeney, Cley, and Weston in Norfolk, Guildford, Godalming, and Farnham in Surrey, Alton, Basingstoke, and Winchester in Hampshire, Petworth in Sussex, and Newbury in Berkshire suggest that these were the places where he traded and from which perhaps he got his cloth.[7]

Bernard Randolph, gentleman. He was described in the pardon roll of 1554 as late of Newark on Trent, ' laborer ', alias late of Ticehurst, Sussex, yeoman, alias late of London, gentleman and esquire.[8] He died between 17 November 1578 and 31 May 1579, and his will describes him as of Stanmore, Middlesex. He left a house, cottage, orchard, and garden in Ticehurst to his son Edmund, a house and land in Ticehurst and a house in Hawkhurst to his son William, and £20 to each of his three daughters, Hester, Judith, and Anne.[9] Randolph must be distinguished from the Bernard Randolph, common serjeant of London, who died 7 August 1583.[10]

Henry Richards. Richards became free of the Drapers Company by apprenticeship in 1529.[11] In 1544 he was apparently trading with Spain, where Thomas Castell was his factor.[12] Later he was importing raisins,

---

[1] *C.P.R. 1550–3*, p. 258 ; J. Latimer, *History of the Society of Merchant Venturers of the City of Bristol*, pp. 22, 38, 42.   [2] Boyd, p. 150 ; Johnson, ii. 471.
[3] Exch. K.R. Port Books, 2/1.
[4] Patent Rolls, 6 Eliz., pt. 12. Lingelbach, *Merchant Adventurers of England*, pp. 231–2, gives the name as Quartes.   [5] Hakluyt, ii. 47.
[6] Ibid., ii. 86.   [7] P.C.C. 3 Langley.   [8] *C.P.R. 1554–5*, pp. 350–1.
[9] P.C.C. 21 Bakon.   [10] *Inq. p.m. Lond.*, iii. 74–5 ; Stow, i. 19, 114.
[11] Boyd, p. 153.   [12] Marsden, i. 126.

probably from Spain,[1] to which he exported cloth,[2] and he was a charter member of the Spanish Company in 1577.[3] Richards died in 1583, leaving a small personal estate to his sister, Elizabeth Buell, his two sons, John and Alexander, and four grandchildren.[4]

John Rivers. Rivers was the son of Richard Rivers of Penshurst, Kent, who was steward of Edward, duke of Buckingham.[5] He was a grocer, alderman, 1565–84, and mayor in 1573–4, when he was knighted; he died about March 1584.[6] Rivers was an assistant of the Merchants Adventurers' Company in 1564,[7] a consul of the Russia Company in 1569,[8] and a charter member of the Spanish Company in 1577.[9] His chief business as a merchant seems to have been the export of cloth.[10] Rivers paid £253 7s. for chantry lands in Kent in 1548 [11] and bought the rectory and advowson of Hadlow, Kent, in 1562.[12] He lent £1500 to the crown in 1569.[13] Rivers left the manor of Chafford, Kent, to his wife Elizabeth, the daughter of Sir George Barne, other lands in Kent to his sons George and John, three houses in London to his son Henry, and a house in Tonbridge, the 'Three Ashes', to his daughter Dorcas. By a codicil he stipulated that certain woods in Kent could be sold for making charcoal and the purchase money divided among his widow, his daughter, and his sons, Henry, Richard, William, and Edward.[14]

Edmund Roberts of Hawkhurst, Kent. Roberts, who may have been a draper,[15] was both a merchant and an industrialist. He seems to have exported beer and cloth and to have traded at both London and Chichester.[16] He was a promoter of the Guinea voyage of 1558.[17] In 1561 he received a pardon for all offences committed in respect of exporting money, plate, corn, victuals, and wood contrary to statutes as well as for offences in connexion with customs duties.[18] As an industrialist Roberts was engaged in the production of iron and steel. He was a charter member of the Mineral and

---

[1] Exch. K.R. Customs Accounts, 86/2.

[2] H.C.A. Examinations, 9 (12 Jan. 1555).

[3] Patent Rolls, 19 Eliz., pt. 8.

[4] P.C.C. 40 Rowe. His bequests came to less than £200, but he left the 'residue' to Elizabeth Buell and his son John.

[5] Strype, ii. bk. v. 135 ; Overall, p. 38 n.

[6] Beaven, ii. 37.   [7] Patent Rolls, 6 Eliz., pt. 12.

[8] Hakluyt, ii. 86.   [9] Patent Rolls, 19 Eliz., pt. 8.

[10] Exch. K.R. Port Books, 2/1 ; S.P.D. Eliz., vi. no. 52 ; Smit, i. 709, 747.

[11] C.P.R. 1548–9, pp. 81–2.   [12] Ibid., 1560–3, p. 546.

[13] Burgon, ii. 343.   [14] P.C.C. 37 Butts.

[15] Boyd, p. 155 ; Johnson, ii. 339.

[16] C.P.R. 1549–51, p. 118 ; Exch. K.R. Customs Accounts, 87/4 ; Smit, ii. 791–2.   [17] H.C.A. Libels, 37. no. 247.   [18] C.P.R. 1560–3, p. 154.

Battery Works [1] and a partner with Sir Henry Sidney and Joan Knight, widow, in steelworks in Kent and ironworks in Glamorgan in 1567. Roberts seems to have had a half share in the iron- and steelworks, but the enterprise was not a success, largely apparently through the competition of imported steel, and shortly after 1572 production ceased.[2] By then Roberts may have been in financial difficulties, for about 1570 he sold the family seat of Elfords, Hawkhurst,[3] and after 1571 he refused to meet the calls on his stock in the Russia Company.[4] Later Roberts was engaged in casting ordnance at Abercarn, Monmouthshire, but about 1580 he was in prison for debt, and 36 pieces of his ordnance had been seized. He died sometime before 1590, intestate and owing £2700.[5]

Francis Robinson. Robinson seems to have been a merchant of the staple,[6] a promotor of the Guinea voyage of 1558,[7] an assistant of the Merchant Adventurers' Company in 1564,[8] and an exporter of wool and cloth.[9] He was probably the collector in London of custom and subsidies on exports who took a lease of the duties on French wines in 1572 and of the new impositions on sweet wines of Spain and the Levant in 1573. His commitments under these leases ' seem to have proved too heavy for him, and some time during 1573 he went bankrupt and died soon after '.[10]

Sir Robert Rochester, knight, comptroller of the household.[11] Rochester, who died unmarried on 28 November 1557, left £100 to the Queen, £50 to the prior of the Black Friars, £20 p.a. to the abbess of Sion, Middlesex, £10 p.a. for a chantry priest at Terling, Essex, £5 p.a. to the prioress of Langley, and lands in Essex to the prior of the House of Jesus in Sheen, Surrey.[12]

William Rose. He may have been the haberdasher of that name who died in October or November 1557, apparently without issue, and who left

---

[1] Carr, p. 19.

[2] *H.M.C. Lord de L'Isle and Dudley*, i. 317–21 ; H.R. Schubert, ' The economic aspect of Sir Henry Sidney's steelworks at Robertsbridge in Sussex, and Boxhurst, in Kent ', *Journal of the Iron and Steel Institute*, vol. 164, pp. 278–80.

[3] Hasted, *Kent*, ed. 1797, vii. 146.   [4] Lans. MSS. 161, no. 95.

[5] Schubert, op. cit. ; E. G. Jones, *Exchequer proceedings (equity) concerning Wales, Henry VIII–Elizabeth*, pp. 257–8.   [6] *C.P.R. 1558–60*, pp. 24, 411.

[7] H.C.A. Libels, 37. no. 247.   [8] Patent Rolls, 6 Eliz., pt. 12.

[9] Exch. K.R. Customs Accounts, 87/4, 7. For Robinson's obscure dealings with George Stoddard, see Hall, *Society in the Elizabethan age*, pp. 53–4.

[10] F. C. Dietz, *English public finance, 1558–1641*, p. 315.

[11] *D.N.B.*, Sir Robert Rochester, 1494?–1557.

[12] P.C.C. F 15 Welles.

100 marks and a gold ring to his wife. Other small bequests included a bow and two dozen arrows to Nicholas Warden and an old feather bed, bolster, and sheets to Joan, the servant of Rose's sister, Katherine Russell.[1]

Sir Richard Sackville, knight.[2]

Thomas Sares. He was probably the haberdasher and cloth exporter [3] who died in 1587 or 1588, leaving tenements in London and land elsewhere to three of his four sons and to his married daughter, Joan Bushe.[4] He also left a personal estate of £359 1s. 9½d.[5]

Blase Saunders. Saunders was Sir Francis Walsingham's cousin, but the exact degree of cousinship is uncertain.[6] In 1547 he was exporting cloth [7] and the following year was engaged in marine insurance.[8] He was a grocer, a merchant of the staple, and a wool exporter.[9] He imported raisins, probably from Spain, from which he was importing soap and Seville oil in 1550, apparently in partnership with Richard Wigmour.[10] He was a charter assistant of the Spanish Company of 1577.[11] Saunders was a charter assistant of the Russia Company and signed the instructions sent out to the company's agents in Russia on 5 May 1560 and 8 May 1561,[12] but he was not, as Professor Conyers Read thought, a governor of the company in 1561,[13] nor does he seem ever to have held that position. In 1570 Saunders received a grant for twenty-one years of the office of Garbler of Spices in London, and on his death, apparently in 1581, Walsingham intervened to protect the interests of his cousin, Saunders's widow, in the unexpired term of the office.[14] Saunders

---

[1] P.C.C. 50 Wrastley.

[2] *D.N.B.*, Sir Richard Sackville, d. 1556. Sackville owned ironworks at Sheffield and Worth in Sussex (P.C.C. 14 Crymes).

[3] Exch. K.R. Customs Accounts, 167/1.   [4] P.C.C. 57 Rutland.

[5] Common Serjeant's Book, i. f. 31d. (Corporation of London Records Office).

[6] C. Read, *Mr. Secretary Walsingham and the policy of Queen Elizabeth*, iii. 370 n. Walsingham's cousin Alice, daughter of Sir Edmund Walsingham, married Thomas Saunders, who may have been Blase's brother or father.

[7] Exch. K.R. Customs Accounts, 167/1.   [8] Marsden, ii. 45–6.

[9] *C.P.R. 1557–8*, p. 300 ; Exch. K.R. Customs Accounts, 87/7 ; Exch. K.R. Port Books, 5/6.

[10] H.C.A. Examinations, 6 (24 April, 13 June 1551). Exch. K.R. Customs Accounts, 86/2.

[11] Patent Rolls, 19 Eliz., pt. 8.   [12] Hakluyt, i. 404–6, ii. 4–9.

[13] Read, op. cit. *C.S.P. Colonial, East Indies, 1513–1616*, p. 4, shows that William Garrard and Thomas Lodge were the governors in 1561.

[14] Overall, pp. 272–3 ; *C.S.P.D. 1581–90*, p. 273.

left a house and tenement in St. Helen, Bishopsgate, a house in Floore, Northants, in which a carpenter dwelt, and all his goods to his wife, Elizabeth.[1]

Drew Saunders. There seems no evidence of what relation, if any, Drew was to Blase Saunders. He was a merchant of the staple [2] and M.P. for Brackley, Northants, in 1558.[3] He died some time before 23 June 1579, leaving 100 marks and part of his dwelling-house, Moorecroftes in Hillingdon, Middlesex, to his wife Anne, who was to be provided with diet for herself and her maid by his executors. He also left 40s. to a servant and kinsman, John Saunders.[4]

Sir Henry Sidney, knight.[5] The *D.N.B.* account of Sidney does not mention his membership of the Russia Company or his ownership of ironworks. According to the account of the first voyage to Russia in 1553, written by Clement Adams, it was Sidney who addressed the assembled merchants and recommended Richard Chancellor to them as pilot major of the voyage. Chancellor had been brought up by Sidney who had ' a full and perfect knowledge of him '.[6] Sidney paid his initial subscription of £25 to the enterprise and met a call of £5 in 1556,[7] but there seems no evidence that he took any further interest in the company. Sidney owned ironworks at Robertsbridge, Sussex, and was a partner with Edmund Roberts and Joan Knight in steelworks in Kent and ironworks in Glamorgan.[8] He was also a member of the Mineral and Battery Works.[9]

Thomas Smith. It is impossible to be sure of Smith's identity, but he was probably the well-known London customs official of that name who died in 1591 and whose son, Sir Thomas Smith, was governor of the Russia Company in 1600 and ambassador to Russia in 1604.[10]

John Southcote, esquire. Southcote, who was a charter consul of the Russia Company, was probably the judge of that name who died in 1585.[11]

Thomas Sparcheforde. He was a cloth exporter in 1547 and 1553-4.[12]

---

[1] P.C.C. 34 Darcy.   [2] *C.P.R. 1557-8*, p. 300.   [3] *Return*, i. 397.
[4] P.C.C. 26 Bakon.   [5] *D.N.B.*, Sir Henry Sidney, 1529-86.
[6] Hakluyt, i. 269-70.   [7] *H.M.C. Lord de L'Isle and Dudley*, i. 254.
[8] Ibid., pp. 305-21.   [9] Carr, p. 18.
[10] *D.N.B.*, Sir Thomas Smith or Smythe, 1558?-1625 ; *H.M.C. Salisbury*, x. 236.   [11] *D.N.B.*, John Southcote, 1511-85.
[12] Exch. K.R. Customs Accounts, 87/4, 167/1.

John Sparke. Sparke was a merchant tailor and cloth exporter.[1] In 1565 he was exporting cloth to Spain [2] and twelve years later he was a member of the Spanish Company.[3] He was said to have 'the Spanishe tounge'.[4] Sparke was a charter assistant of the Russia Company [5] and was employed by the company in Russia and Persia. In 1566 he made a journey by water from Kholmogory to Novgorod [6] and two years later was one of the company's servants in Persia.[7] He was in Moscow in 1571 when part of the city was burned by the Tartars and some of the company's servants perished in the fire. Sparke took refuge in a cellar of the company's house and escaped destruction.[8] He died about 1580, leaving lands at Bradwell, Essex, and elsewhere to his daughter Judith, who had married John Davenant, merchant tailor, in 1563.[9] To Davenant, Sparke left his 'freedome of Muscovy and newe trades', and to Davenant's son, John, he left his bed with coverings and a small table diamond.[10]

Robert Spencer. He was probably a cloth exporter.[11]

Richard Springham. Springham seems to have been a mercer, a merchant adventurer, and a cloth exporter.[12] He married a sister of Thomas Nicholes the elder,[13] and he and Nicholes were executors of the will of Lady Locke, widow of Sir William Locke, in 1551.[14] Under Mary, Springham became an exile on the continent, where he helped to finance his fellow-exiles and where he stayed from the winter of 1556-7 to the spring of 1559.[15] On his return to England, Springham resumed his trading activities. He was exporting cloth in 1559 [16] and was a charter member of the Merchant Adventurers' Company in 1564.[17] Four years later he was a member of the Mines Royal in which he was still a shareholder in 1580.[18] In addition to these activities, Springham was a shipowner and an insurer of ships and their cargoes.[19]

Robert Srokhey.

---

[1] Ibid., 167/1 ; Clode, ii. 341–3. [2] Exch. K.R. Port Books, 2/1.
[3] Patent Rolls, 19 Eliz., pt. 8. [4] Morgan and Coote, ii. 222.
[5] He was also an assistant in 1569 (Hakluyt, ii. 86).
[6] Hakluyt, ii. 57–65. [7] Ibid., ii. 108–19.
[8] Morgan and Coote, ii. 338–9. [9] Machyn, p. 300.
[10] P.C.C. 5 Darcy. [11] Exch. K.R. Customs Accounts, 87/4, 167/1.
[12] Ibid. ; *C.P.R. 1553-4*, p. 425 ; Smit, i. 757. [13] P.C.C. 3 Streat.
[14] Machyn, p. 323. [15] C. H. Garrett, *The Marian exiles*, pp. 292–3.
[16] S.P.D. Eliz., vi. no. 52. [17] Patent Rolls, 6 Eliz., pt. 12.
[18] Collingwood, *Elizabethan Keswick*, pp. 3–4, where he is described as alderman, but there seems to have been no alderman of that name.
[19] H.C.A. Examinations, 14 (2 March 1562), 15 (25 June 1564).

Thomas Standbridge. He was importing unspecified goods in 1553–4.[1]

Thomas Starke, draper. Thomas Starke or Starkey was bound apprentice to a draper in 1537 and belonged to the livery of the Drapers Company by 1556.[2] He seems to have employed a clothworker, Robert Housse,[3] and to have exported cloth and imported alum and canvas.[4] Starke, who apparently died about 1564,[5] must be distinguished from Thomas Starkey, skinner and alderman, whose will was proved on 22 January 1594.[6]

John Starkey. He was probably the mercer who was trading to Chios sometime between 1533 and 1544 [7] and who died before 1567. His daughter Elizabeth, who married John Nelthorpe of Stepney, had in 1567 the reversion of three messuages and a garden in East Greenwich after the death of Joan, widow of Thomas Starkey; this suggests that he was related to Thomas.[8]

John Staunton.

Edmund Stile. Stile may have been a Suffolk man for he owned property in that county and was brought up at Hadleigh.[9] He was a grocer, an exporter of cloth, and an importer of figs, sugar, almonds, madder, and linen.[10] He died in February or March 1564, apparently without issue. He left his ' headhouse ' at Ipswich, lands in Suffolk, and four tenements and a house with garden and henyard in London to his wife Anne. Stile had also a considerable personal estate from which he left £100 to the poor and £60 to the hospitals in London, £20 to the poor of Ipswich, £6 13s. 4d. to the poor of Hadleigh, £20 to the Grocers Company, and £4 to John a Baye, who came out of Flanders and whom he had brought up in his house ' for God his sake '. His bequests to relatives included £20 to his brother-in-law Richard Lambert, grocer, and £100 equally among the four sons of his late cousin, Humphrey Stile.[11]

William Strete. He was probably a draper who died in 1557 [12] leaving his goods to his wife Anne, the fur off his best gown and his best black jacket

---

1 Exch. K.R. Customs Accounts, 86/2.

2 Boyd, p. 174 ; Johnson, ii. 407.

3 Hall, *Society in the Elizabethan age*, p. 52.

4 Exch. K.R. Customs Accounts, 86/2, 6, 87/4, 167/1.

5 Boyd, p. 174.   6 Beaven, ii. 40 ; P.C.C. 3 Darcy.   7 Hakluyt, iii. 6.

8 Hasted, p. 107.   9 P.C.C. 7 Stevenson.

10 Exch. K.R. Customs Accounts, 86/2, 4, 87/4, 167/1.

11 P.C.C. 7 Stevenson.

12 Boyd, p. 177. His identity is not certain for there was a William Strete, merchant of the staple, who was alive in 1558 (*C.P.R. 1557–8*, p. 300).

to his brother-in-law, Richard Thomas, the outside of the gown to Thomas's wife, and the remission of a year's service to his apprentice, Arnold Champion.[1]

Richard Taylor. He may have been the grocer and cloth exporter [2] who died in 1563, leaving property in London, Kent, and Yorkshire to his wife Edith with reversion to his eldest son, Richard. He also left £100 to each of his four sons and two daughters and £2 to each of his two apprentices, Thomas Gittons and Thomas Smith, who were to be faithful servants to his widow and were to have the occupying of the portions of two of his children. In addition Gittons was relieved of one year's service as apprentice.[3]

Clement Throckmorton, esquire. Clement Throckmorton of Haseley, Warwickshire, was the son of Sir George Throckmorton by his wife Katherine, the daughter of Nicholas, lord Vaux of Harrowden.[4] He was a courtier and several times M.P. for Warwick county and borough.[5] Throckmorton was buying monastic property in the fifteen-forties [6] and chantry lands in the fifteen-fifties.[7] In 1550 he leased an iron furnace at Worth from the crown for twenty-one years at a rent of £90 p.a.[8] He was an assistant of the Russia Company in 1569,[9] and died in 1573. His eldest son Job, who inherited Haseley manor, was a puritan and friend of Thomas Cartwright.[10]

John Traves. Traves was a merchant tailor,[11] a merchant adventurer,[12] and a cloth exporter.[13] He died 19 February 1570, leaving his dwelling-house, which had been made out of five tenements, and a tenement to his second wife, Elizabeth, and her heirs for ever, and a messuage with shops and cellars to Elizabeth for life with reversion to his son Edmund. He also left £50 to each of his eleven children, of whom four were the children of his first marriage.[14]

Martin Trewennour.

William Tucker. He was perhaps the grocer who was unsuccessfully nominated for alderman in 1555.[15]

---

[1] P.C.C. 15 Wrastley.
[2] Exch. K.R. Customs Accounts, 87/4.   [3] P.C.C. 37 Chayre.
[4] G. Lipscomb, *History and antiquities of the county of Buckingham*, iv. 399–400.
[5] *Return*, i. 373, 377, 380, 383, 406, 411.
[6] *Letters and Papers, Henry VIII*, xx. pt. i. 129, 664–5.
[7] *C.P.R. 1553*, pp. 28–9.
[8] E. Straker, *Wealden iron*, pp. 463–4.   [9] Hakluyt, ii. 86.
[10] A. F. Scott Pearson, *Thomas Cartwright and Elizabethan Puritanism*, p. 303.
[11] Clode, i. 229, ii. 342.   [12] Patent Rolls, 6 Eliz., pt. 12.
[13] Exch. K.R. Customs Accounts, 87/4, 90/11 ; Exch. K.R. Port Books, 2/1.
[14] P.C.C. 9 Lyon ; *Inq. p.m. Lond.*, ii. 148–50   [15] Beaven, ii. 25, 227.

Geoffrey Vaughan. Vaughan was born at Oswestry, Shropshire, about 1510 and came to London at the age of 20, where he became a merchant tailor [1] and shipowner. In 1553 he owned the *Christopher Bennett*, which was later lost on a Guinea voyage, and the *Hart*,[2] and in 1556 he was part owner of a ship engaged in trade with Spain.[3] He was a promoter of the Guinea voyage of 1558.[4] In 1560 Vaughan was concerned with furnishing ships with ordnance, victuals, and men for service in Scottish waters,[5] and on 24 December 1560 he was appointed to the 'office of an assistant of the chief officers of the admiralty and marine causes.'[6] Later he was apparently engaged in victualling the forces in Ireland.[7]

Henry Vinar. Vinar, who was a mercer,[8] was exporting cloth and importing hats in the fifteen-fifties when he shared with Lionel Duckett a licence to import felts or hats from Spain and Portugal.[9] He was an assistant of the Merchant Adventurers' Company in 1564 [10] and was exporting cloth to Antwerp the following year.[11]

Sir Edward Waldegrave, knight, master of the wardrobe.[12]

Geoffrey Walkeden. Walkeden was a skinner and was twice master of the Skinners Company.[13] He was an exporter of cloth to Antwerp, from which he imported linen,[14] and a promotor of the Guinea voyage of 1558.[15] Walkeden was a charter assistant of the Russia Company and an assistant of the Merchant Adventurers' Company in 1564.[16]

William Watson. Watson, who was a charter assistant of the Russia Company, cannot be identified with certainty. He was probably the William Watson who was apprenticed to a draper in 1513 [17] and was a royal agent or merchant under Henry VIII, Edward VI, Mary, and Elizabeth, when he was chiefly engaged in buying naval materials at Danzig.[18] Apart from his

---

[1] Clode, i. 249, ii. 344 ; H.C.A. Examinations, 12 (25 Jan. 1560).

[2] Blake, ii. 430 ; H.C.A. Examinations, 9 (9 June 1554).

[3] Marsden, ii. 97–8.   [4] H.C.A. Libels, 37. no. 247.

[5] C.S.P. For. 1559–60, pp. 331, 379, 392.   [6] C.P.R. 1560–3, p. 64.

[7] H.M.C. Lord de L'Isle and Dudley, i. 409.   [8] C.P.R. 1553–4, p. 439.

[9] Exch. K.R. Customs Accounts, 86/6, 87/4 ; S.P.D. Eliz., vi. no. 52 ; Chancery Proceedings, Second Series, 50. no. 93.

[10] Patent Rolls, 6 Eliz., pt. 12.   [11] Exch. K.R. Port Books, 2/1.

[12] D.N.B., Sir Edward Waldegrave, 1517?–61.   [13] Lambert, pp. 237, 376.

[14] Exch. K.R. Port Books, 2/1, 4/2.   [15] H.C.A. Libels, 37. no. 247.

[16] Patent Rolls, 6 Eliz., pt. 12.   [17] Boyd, p. 195.

[18] A.P.C. 1542–7, p. 321 ; 1547–50, pp. 120, 223 ; 1554–6, p. 236 ; Machyn, p. 218.

official employment, he seems to have been a shipowner [1] and a cloth exporter.[2]   He died on 20 November 1559.[3]   According to his will, Watson was born in Shropshire and he left £6 13s. 4d. for marriage portions for poor maidens in that county.   He also left 516 oz. of plate to his second wife, Anne, by whom he had seven children.   The plate had been inherited from Anne's mother, Elizabeth Ouley.[4]

Sir Thomas White, knight and alderman.[5]   White's benefactions are well known,[6] but there seems little evidence of his business activities. He was apparently trading with Antwerp in 1546 [7] and was importing wine in 1553–4.[8]   He was trading with Barbary in 1555 and again in 1559 and he maintained a factor there.[9]   White was a charter assistant of the Russia Company and he left his 'freedom of Moscovia' to his apprentice, Gilbert Moxsey.   If Moxsey refused it, the freedom could go to any of White's apprentices who would accept it.[10]   It is said that White suffered from the falling off in the cloth trade after 1562 and that he died a poor man.[11]   The evidence for these statements is not clear.   White died without issue on 11 February 1567, leaving some 60 messuages, shops, and tenements in London value £115 12s. 8d p.a. to his wife Joan for life, with reversion to St. John's College, Oxford.[12]

Elizabeth Wilford, widow.   She was exporting cloth in 1553–4.[13]   It is not clear whose widow she was.   She was not the widow of the John Wilford, merchant tailor, who died in 1551.   It is just possible that she was the widow of Alexander Woodfoord, who was a merchant on the *Bona Esperanza* in the voyage to Russia of 1553 and who presumably perished when the ship was frozen in the White Sea.[14]

John Wilford, the younger.   He seems to have been the second son of John Wilford, the elder, a merchant tailor who died in February or March 1551, leaving property in London and Surrey to his three sons and an annuity of £50 to his widow Mary.[15]   It is possible that he was an exile at Frankfort during part of Mary's reign.[16]   He was a cloth exporter.[17]

[1] *A.P.C. 1542–7*, pp. 374, 376.

[2] Exch. K.R. Customs Accounts, 87/4, 167/1.   [3] *Inq. p.m. Lond.*, i. 203.

[4] P.C.C. 4 Mellershe.   [5] *D.N.B.*, Sir Thomas White, 1492–1567.

[6] For an account of them and of White see Clode, ii. chs. x–xii, xiv.

[7] H. Ellis, *Original Letters*, Second Series, ii. 175.

[8] Exch. K.R. Customs Accounts, 86/2.   [9] Blake, ii. 347–8, 433–40.

[10] P.C.C. 36 Stonarde.   [11] *D.N.B.*   [12] *Inq. p.m. Lond.*, ii. 105–9.

[13] Exch. K.R. Customs Accounts, 87/4.   [14] Hakluyt, i. 244.

[15] P.C.C. 9 Bucke.   [16] C. H. Garrett, *The Marian exiles*, pp. 332–3.

[17] Exch. K.R. Customs Accounts, 87/4, 167/1.

Richard Wilkes.[1] He was probably the merchant tailor who died in 1560, leaving property in London value £27 p.a. to his son John, and £10, 5 pairs of sheets, a tablecloth and 6 napkins to his apprentice Thomas Nicholls.[2]

Thomas Wilkes. Wilkes seems to have been a haberdasher, a merchant of the staple, and a cloth exporter.[3] He was elected sheriff in 1551 but refused to serve on the grounds that he was ' not of ability nor substance for the said office' as he was 'in debt for a purchase of landes above sixe thousand poundes'.[4] He paid the fine of £200 for not serving. Wilkes was chosen alderman in 1558, but was apparently never sworn. He died in January 1559.[5]

John Wilkinson. Wilkinson seems to have been a merchant tailor[6] and he may have been the ' Master Wilkinson' who supplied six pieces of 'open lace of soundery collors' for export to Russia in 1567.[7] His widow Mary died on 21 December 1573 leaving two messuages in London to her younger sons, Roger and Paul.[8]

William, marquis of Winchester, lord high treasurer.[9]

Robert Wolman. Wolman was a mercer, a cloth exporter in 1553–4 and 1559,[10] and an assistant of the Russia Company in 1569.[11] He died without issue in January 1571, leaving lands in Cambridgeshire to his wife Margery and property in London and Middlesex for the building of a school at Uxbridge and for endowing the master with a salary of 20 marks p.a. Wolman left his freedom of the Russia Company to his cousin John Kent. He also left 20 marks to Anne Langham, a poor maid whom he had brought up from infancy for charity's sake, and £6 13s. 4d. to Jane, the daughter of William Loddington, mercer, which Jane had ' a brent face '.[12]

Sir Thomas Woodhouse, knight. Sir Thomas was a Norfolk landowner who was dealing extensively in monastic, chantry, and other property

---

[1] The name is also spelt Willes in the charter.

[2] P.C.C. 25 Mellershe. The property included the Black Swan in Holborn.

[3] *C.P.R. 1553–4*, p. 414 ; Exch. K.R. Customs Accounts, 167/1.

[4] Wriothesley, *Chronicle*, ii. 51, 54. He had bought chantry property in London in 1548 (*C.P.R. 1547–8*, pp. 384–5).

[5] Beaven, ii. 36.   [6] Clode, ii. 342.

[7] Johnson, ii. 457.   [8] *Inq. p.m. Lond.*, ii. 173–4.

[9] *D.N.B.*, Sir William Paulet, first marquis of Winchester, 1485?–1572.

[10] Exch. K.R. Customs Accounts, 87/4 ; S.P.D. Eliz., vi. no. 52.

[11] Hakluyt, ii. 86.   [12] P.C.C. 8 Holney.

in the fifteen-forties and fifteen-fifties.[1] He was supplying victuals for the king's use at Calais, Boulogne, and elsewhere in 1547 [2] and held a licence for the export of 6000 quarters of grain the following year.[3] He was M.P. for Great Yarmouth in 1558 and 1559,[4] and on 19 May 1559 the corporation granted him 40s. p.a. for life for the goodwill and friendship which he bore to the town.[5] At that time Woodhouse was importing salt, fish, wine, prunes, and vinegar at Great Yarmouth.[6] He died about 1571 leaving £40 to his maid, Anne Bishop, 100 ewes to his nephew John Shelton, and property and money to his nephews, Thomas and Henry, and his nieces, Elizabeth and Margaret, the children of Sir William Woodhouse.[7]

Sir William Woodhouse, knight. Sir William was a Norfolk landowner and the younger brother of Sir Thomas, with whom he was associated in the buying and selling of property.[8] He was appointed master of the ordnance of the king's ships in 1546 [9] and lieutenant of the admiralty of England in 1552, an office which he vacated under Mary.[10] He was a viceadmiral in 1558.[11] Woodhouse was M.P. for Great Yarmouth in 1545, 1547, and 1553 and for Norfolk in 1558 and 1563.[12] He died in 1564 or 1565 leaving manors in Norfolk and Suffolk to his eldest son Thomas, £100 to each of his daughters Elizabeth and Margaret, and a short gown of velvet and a velvet cap with gold buttons, given to him by the earl of Leicester, to his son-in-law Philip Parker.[13]

David Woodroff, alderman. Woodroff was the son of John Woodroff of Ashcombe, Devon.[14] He was a haberdasher, and an alderman from 1548 to 1560 ; he died on 24 March 1563 after a long illness.[15] Woodroff was a merchant of the staple and an exporter of wool and cloth.[16] He left three

---

[1] *Letters and Papers, Henry VIII*, xxi. pt. i. 570 ; *C.P.R. 1548–9*, pp. 112–18 ; *1549–51*, p. 322 ; *1550–3*, pp. 29–31.   [2] *A.P.C. 1547–50*, p. 78.
[3] *C.P.R. 1553*, p. 401.   [4] *Return*, i. 397, 401.
[5] C. G. Bayne, ' The first house of commons of Queen Elizabeth ', *E.H.R.*, xxiii. 674.   [6] Smit, ii. 812.   [7] P.C.C. 18 Daper.
[8] *C.P.R. 1548–9*, p. 86 ; *1550–3*, pp. 29–31.
[9] *Letters and Papers, Henry VIII*, xxi. pt. i. 356.
[10] *C.P.R. 1550–3*, p. 404 ; Williamson, *Sir John Hawkins*, p. 323.
[11] *A.P.C. 1556–8*, p. 235.
[12] *Return*, i. 376, 379, 397, 405, Appendix. xxxi.
[13] P.C.C. 6 Morison. Parker may have been Woodhouse's stepson, not his son-in-law as the will describes him, for Woodhouse married an Elizabeth Parker (*C.P.R. 1550–3*, p. 329).
[14] Machyn, p. 395.   [15] Beaven, ii. 32, 210.
[16] *C.P.R. 1553–4*, p. 415 ; Exch. K.R. Customs Accounts, 87/7, 167/1 ; S.P.D. Eliz., vi. no. 52.

houses and four tenements in London, a house at Barnet, two houses at St Albans, and a pasture at Enfield to his wife Elizabeth for life with reversion to his sons Nicholas, Stephen, and Richard.   Nicholas had already received £266 13s. 4d. at the time of his marriage, as had his sister Elizabeth.   Woodroff also left £20 for bringing water to Bishopsgate, and four cartloads of great coals p.a. for twenty years for the poor of Lime Street ward.[1]   His son Stephen was a merchant, exporting cloth to the continent in 1573.[2]

Nicholas Wotton, clerk, doctor in civil law.[3]

William Wotton, gentleman. He seems to have been M.P. for Maidstone in 1553 and for Gatton in 1554.[4]   He died towards the end of 1556, leaving property at Hadlow and Brenchley in Kent to his wife Mary for life with reversion to his brother Thomas.[5]

Sir Thomas Wroth, knight.[6]   Wroth's membership of the Russia Company was rather unusual, for he must have been a charter member *in absentia*. Wroth was implicated in Suffolk's rising and escaped to the continent, where he arrived at Padua on 10 July 1554. He remained on the continent until the end of 1558,[7] and cannot therefore have been in England when the charter was granted to the company on 26 February 1555. He was presumably a subscriber to the voyage of 1553, which may account for his membership two years later. Wroth died a rich man in 1573. He left manors in Middlesex, Essex, and Somerset, some of which went to his wife Mary, the daughter of Lord Rich, for life with reversion to his eldest son Richard, who seems to have inherited the remainder.   Wroth also left £500 to each of his six younger sons, of whom Edward was bound apprentice to a merchant and was to receive £300 of his £500 within a year after his apprenticeship ' for his better credit and furtherance in the trade or traffic of merchandize '. Wroth's three married daughters received £20 each and his four unmarried daughters £400 each with an additional £40 each for their wedding apparel and wedding dinner. By a codicil the four unmarried daughters received an additional £60 each, which in the case of the three eldest of them was a reward for the care they had taken of their father, especially during his last illness. Wroth took elaborate precautions for the safe keeping of the money which he left. A strong chest with four locks was to be bought and was to stand in the house of his loving friend, Peter Osborne. Each of

---

[1] P.C.C. 21 Chayre ; *Inq. p.m. Lond.*, ii. 12–14.

[2] H.C.A. Examinations, 20 (31 Oct. 1573).

[3] *D.N.B.*, Nicholas Wotton, 1497?–1567.

[4] *Return*, i. 379, 391.   [5] P.C.C. 24 Ketchyn.

[6] *D.N.B.*, Sir Thomas Wroth, 1516–73.

[7] C. H. Garrett, *The Marian exiles*, pp. 344–6.

the four executors, who included Osborne, was to have a key, which presumably opened only one of the locks, so that none of them could open the chest without the consent of all. Into the chest was to be put the money which came to the executors.[1]

Sir John York, knight.[2] The account of York in the *D.N.B.* says little about his trading activities. He was a charter assistant of the Russia Company and a promoter of the Barbary voyage of 1552 [3] and of the Guinea voyages of 1553 and 1554.[4] He was trading with Barbary again in 1555.[5] York was exporting cloth in 1547, 1553-4, and in 1559.[6] He was importing aniseed, pepper, mace, and nutmegs from Antwerp in 1568.[7] His will was proved on 2 February 1569. In it he left property in London and Yorkshire to his six sons and 1000 marks to his daughter Jane.[8]

Richard Young,[9] **gentleman.** Young, who had become an assistant of the Russia Company by 1569,[10] was apparently a grocer [11] and a London customs official. He seems to have held the office of packer of London from about 1550.[12] In or about 1571 he and Sir Richard Martin took a lease of the wine duties, but they surrendered the lease without making any attempt to work it.[13] Later Young was a subscriber to Frobisher's voyages to the north-west and was one of the commissioners appointed to test the ore which Frobisher brought back with him.[14] At that time Young was a customer of London.[15] In 1588 Young received the notorious patent for making starch, which was transferred to Sir John Packington in 1594.[16] Young seems to have died in 1595 heavily in debt to the crown, though it was said that he had enjoyed an income of £200 p.a. from lands and leases and had married a widow worth £3000 at least.[17]

---

[1] P.C.C. 16 Pyckering. [2] *D.N.B.*, Sir John York, d. 1569?.
[3] Hakluyt, iv. 33.
[4] Ibid., p. 47 ; Williamson, *Sir John Hawkins*, p. 40.
[5] Blake, ii. 347-8.
[6] Exch. K.R. Customs Accounts, 87/4, 167/1 ; S.P.D. Eliz., vi. no. 52.
[7] Exch. K.R. Port Books, 4/2.   [8] P.C.C. 4 Sheffeld.
[9] The name is also spelt Yong and Yonge.
[10] Hakluyt, ii. 86.   [11] *C.P.R. 1553-4*, p. 418.
[12] *C.S.P.D. 1595-7*, pp. 103-5 ; Strype, i. bk. ii. 51.
[13] F. C. Dietz, *English public finance, 1558–1641*, pp. 314-15.
[14] *C.S.P. Colonial., East Indies, 1513–1616*, pp. 23, 31, 33-4, 37 ; *A.P.C. 1577-8*, pp. 135-6.   [15] *C.S.P.D. 1595-7*, pp. 103-5.
[16] W. H. Price, *The English patents of monopoly*, p. 15 n.
[17] *C.S.P.D. 1595-7*, pp. 103-5 ; *H.M.C. Salisbury*, v. 532-3. The widow may have been Catherine Gough, who married a Richard Young, gentleman, on 28 June 1566 (*Collectanea Topographica*, v. 212).

Walter Young. Young seems to have been a merchant tailor who was trading with Barbary in 1555.[1] It is possible that he later lived and traded in the Azores.[2]

---

[1] Blake, ii. 347–8 ; Clode, i. 362, ii. 340.
[2] *A.P.C. 1586–7,* p. 378.

INDEX OF PERSONS
AND PLACES